THE ULTIMATE CARDINALS RECORD BOOK

A Complete Guide to
the Most Unusual, Unbelievable,
and Unbreakable Records
in Cardinals History

DAN MOORE

TRIUMPH
BOOKS

For my parents, who offered means and motive
to spend my formative years lost in box scores.

This book is available in quantity at special discounts for your group or organization. For further information, contact:

Triumph Books LLC
542 South Dearborn Street
Suite 750
Chicago, Illinois 60605
(312) 939-3330
Fax (312) 663-3557
www.triumphbooks.com

Printed in U.S.A.
ISBN: 978-1-60078-698-3

Design by Patricia Frey

Photos courtesy of AP Images unless otherwise indicated.

CONTENTS

A NOTE ON NUMBERS

The statistics contained in this book are Cardinals team records unless otherwise specified. Following is a legend of commonly used abbreviations in table formats.

1B: Singles
2B: Doubles
3B: Triples
AB: At-Bats
BA: Batting Average
BB: Bases on Balls
CG: Complete Games
ERA: Earned Run Average
ERR: Errors
GF: Games Finished
GP: Games Pitched
GS: Games Started
H: Hits
HBP: Hit by Pitch
HR: Home Runs
IBB: Intentional Bases on Balls
IP: Innings Pitched
K: Strikes
L: Losses
ND: No Decision
OBP: On-Base Percentage
OPS: On-Base and Slugging Percentage
R: Runs
RBI: Runs Batted In
SB: Stolen Bases
SF: Sacrifice Flies
SHO: Shutouts
SLG: Slugging Percentage
SO: Strikeouts
SV: Saves
W: Wins
W–L: Won–Lost
WP: Winning Percentage
XBH: Extra-Base Hit

ACKNOWLEDGMENTS

Many of the statistics in this book would be lost without the brilliant work of Baseball-Reference.com. Sources for historical information include, in addition to a series of increasingly dusty books and microfilm cabinets, the Baseball Almanac (baseball-almanac.com), This Game of Games (thisgameofgames.blogspot.com), and BaseballLibrary.com.

INTRODUCTION

St. Louis has always been a baseball town.

The "Best Fans in Baseball" shtick might be a recent invention, and the Clydesdales haven't always trotted an arc around the outfield, but from the dawn of professional baseball St. Louis has been in love with its players and its team. It's loved baseball so much that owners have permanently sabotaged their hometown team to move there; it's loved baseball so much that it stuck around for 100-game losers, stadiums with ingrown dog tracks, 3'7" pinch-hitters, winners and losers, teams that didn't hit any home runs, teams that only hit home runs, and—most recently—a team that looked dead in the water and suddenly wasn't.

The story of Cardinals baseball is the story of that love affair. It's the story of Rogers Hornsby dominating the National League, making nothing but enemies, and gruffly telling the world that when there was no baseball he did nothing but wait for spring. It's the story of Dizzy Dean and the Gashouse Gang upending baseball decorum, telling tall tales about themselves, and winning the World Series anyway. Later on it's teams and players that act like you wish everybody would—Stan Musial's understated, unassuming brilliance or Bob Gibson's competitive intensity or Ozzie Smith's showmanship.

It's the story, even, of all the strange non-entities that led up to those stories—the Browns of the 1880s that fought and caroused and gambled and, while they were at it, lost an early version of the World Series by the improbable score of 10 games to 5; the St. Louis millionaire who founded his own league and stocked his own team with all the best players; the hapless American League Browns that squandered a chance to be St. Louis' team and rode off into a sunset filled with Bill Veeck's unlikely gimmicks.

It's the story, finally, of thousands of men who, for at least a few days, wore the Birds on the Bat in front of thousands of Cardinals fans and tried to do something unforgettable.

Lots of those men and lots of those fans are gone now, but the numbers they left behind tell those famous Cardinals' stories. It's one thing to know Stan Musial hustled out of the batter's box like nobody else, and another to know that Stan Musial, never known for his speed, hit 177 triples. Lou Brock was fast, but it's his single-season 118 and career 938 stolen bases that tell us how fast. Bob Gibson wasn't just good, he was 1.12.

This book, then, is story all the way through. Some of the stories are written out, and others are included here in the beautiful shorthand baseball has developed over 150 years—30 HR, 100 RBIs, .300 BA, 20 or 300 W. Taken together, they offer a history of the most successful franchise in the National League through 11 championships, innumerable successes and failures, and an impossible number of remarkable sidelines and diversions.

Chapter 1

Albert Pujols Ties Stan the Man with Three MVPs

Cardinals' Career Batting Leaders

Albert Pujols picked a bad time to put together 10 consecutive MVP-caliber seasons. In 2001, the 21-year-old infielder hit .329 with 37 home runs and 130 RBIs, one of the best rookie seasons in the history of baseball. Unfortunately, that same year Barry Bonds also assembled one of the best seasons in the history of baseball, hitting 73 home runs and walking 177 times.

The 2002 season brought more of the same—an even better season from Barry Bonds and for Pujols another second-place finish. In 2003 and 2004, Pujols hit a combined .345 with 89 home runs and 247 RBIs and was unfortunate enough to see Bonds hit 90 home runs and put together an astonishing .609 on-base percentage in 2004.

There just wasn't any way around Barry Bonds, who for four years seemed only to be getting better. Then in 2005, Bonds finally, briefly showed his age. Knee surgery in March left him contemplating retirement, and the Cardinals' 25-year-old slugger, newly installed at first base after a trip around the diamond, had his first clean shot at being named the National League's Most Valuable Player.

That year he did exactly what he always

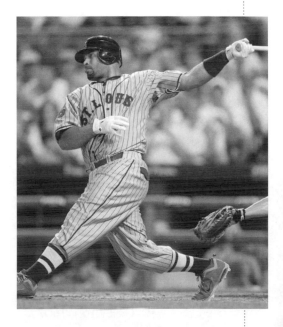

did—he was Albert Pujols. For the third year in a row he led the league in runs scored, hit at least .330, hit at least 40 home runs, and added 117 RBIs. While he was at it, he stole 16 bases and was only caught twice, after having never stolen more than five in a season before.

That year being Albert Pujols was his best asset, but as he added to his awards cabinet it became less beneficial each year—after a while the voters grew tired of handing Pujols the Most Valuable Player award simply for being

Unbreakable?

No National Leaguer has accumulated more hits for a single team than Stan Musial's 3,630.

the most valuable player in the National League.

The voters seemed to thrill at each new chance to hand the award to some one-year-wonder or the lynchpin of some surprise contender. In the course of winning his three NL MVP Awards—tied with Stan Musial for

Redbird Reference

Joe Medwick

"Ducky Joe" doesn't sound quite right, nickname-wise, for a bruising slugger who once hit 64 doubles and elsewhere earned the nickname "Muscles" for his physique, but it makes more sense, at least at first, once you understand that Ducky Joe Medwick was short for "Ducky Wucky." Medwick, a 10-time All-Star and the last National Leaguer to earn the Triple Crown, was the most fearsome slugger in the Gashouse Gang and one of the most dangerous hitters to ever undress a third baseman.

He was named "Ducky" apparently for his bowlegged saunter, but it was his 1937 season that earned him immortality. That year Medwick hit .374 and drove in a league-high 154 RBIs—a brilliant season even for Medwick but nothing too out of the ordinary. It was his 31 home runs, 10 more than he'd ever hit again in a season, that earned him the Triple Crown and the MVP award.

For the most part Ducky Wucky—Muscles, if you were anywhere near him—was perfectly happy to hit doubles, and his 64 in 1936 remains the highest single-season total in National League history.

Contemporary Comparo: An occasionally surly slugger who terrified infielders with his line-drive swing, Ducky Joe at his best might have looked something like Gary Sheffield.

most in team history—Pujols ran into competition from a few types of player, all of them frustrating, none as valuable. For instance:

The Andruw Jones Type: In 2005, Pujols found himself in competition with Andruw Jones despite an on-base percentage 83 points higher than the Braves' increasingly immobile center fielder. The Andruw Jones Type puts up great career-best stats, often leading the league in home runs or RBIs while he's never done it before and will probably never do it again. The surprise doesn't quite curdle over into a fluke since he's always been so talented.

In 2005, Pujols had two Andruw Joneses on his tail. The first one, Jones himself, had managed to combine—for one weird moment—his usual Gold Glove defense with Dave Kingman's plate approach. That year he clubbed a career-high 51 home runs; the voters might have

Behind the Numbers

The Cardinals have had two Triple Crown winners—players who led the league in batting average, home runs, and RBIs in the same season—Rogers Hornsby, who did it in 1922 and 1925, and Joe Medwick, whose Triple Crown in 1937 was the last one accomplished in the National League.

Unbreakable?

Rogers Hornsby's career batting average of .359 is second in baseball history, and the top right-handed mark of all time. Only one other right-hander is in the top 10.

been loath to overlook his .263 batting average except he also led the NL with 128 RBIs.

That was competition enough for Pujols, who still had to contend with the stars on his own team for recognition. But there was more. Closer to home, Derrek Lee had put up a vintage Albert Pujols season for the Cubs, leading the league in batting average and slugging percentage and hitting 99 extra-base hits. Chicago's first baseman had a fair case for the MVP himself, but Pujols' defense and the voters' pent-up desire to crown the Cardinal gave him a narrow victory over Jones.

Sometimes the Andruw Jones Type got the best of Pujols. In 2007 he finished ninth despite leading the league in Wins Above Replacement, a popular sabermetric stat; Jimmy Rollins, the Phillies' popular and omnipresent shortstop, won the MVP thanks to his unlikely run at 30 home runs.

The Ryan Howard Type: In 2006 Pujols' MVP arch nemesis emerged. Ryan Howard, the Phillies' hulking first baseman—

himself a St. Louis native—hit 58 home runs in his first full season, combining it with his only .300 batting average. The sheer counting stats were enough to convince the voters, who gave him 20 first-place votes to Pujols' 12.

Pujols, who hit a career-high 49 home runs himself, actually topped Howard in on-base and slugging percentage, but when confronted with a Ryan Howard Type the voters tended to forget about the things that made Pujols better than the garden-variety slugger.

Defense was usually the first thing to go. Pujols was one of the best defensive first basemen

Redbird Reference

Chick Hafey

Ask any Cardinals fan to name the team's Hall of Famers and they'll name the greats one after the other—Stan Musial, Rogers Hornsby, Bob Gibson, Ozzie Smith, Lou Brock, and so on. Ask a particularly dedicated Cardinals fan and he'll add the next set, your Jim Bottomleys and Joe Medwicks and Enos Slaughters.

Even if your friend can get all the way down to Jesse Haines, he might not remember to tick the box next to the name of Chick Hafey, a forgotten great and as curious a Hall of Famer as you're likely to find. Between 1927 and 1931 Hafey was one of the most dangerous hitters in the National League; plagued by inconsistent hitting before and health problems after, he played 1,283 games in a career that saw him play 100 games in a season just seven times.

A converted pitcher with an incredibly strong arm and a line-drive swing that produced as many as 85 extra-base hits in a season, Hafey emerged as a full-time player the year after the Cardinals' first World Series championship, hitting .329 and leading the National League in slugging percentage.

Hafey, who became one of the first players to wear glasses on the field when sinus problems weakened his eyesight, won the batting title on the last day of the season in 1931, hitting .349 and leading the Cardinals to their second championship with a six-game win over Philadelphia. After holding out for a raise, Branch Rickey traded Hafey just before Opening Day in 1932, but the recurrence of his sinus problems prematurely ended his career in Cincinnati. He was elected to the Hall of Fame in 1971.

Contemporary Comparo: A burly outfielder with a line drive swing and surprising skill on the base paths, Hafey looks a lot like Matt Holliday, if you squint.

of his generation, literally a third baseman trapped at the position by arm injuries, and at his best the difference between his incredible reaction time and gutsy decision-making and Ryan Howard's unremarkable bagsmanship was upwards of 20 runs, according to most advanced defensive statistics.

Pujols' incredible plate discipline usually went, too. From 2005 to 2009, Pujols walked 507 times against just 291 strikeouts. Howard walked 404 times and struck out an incredible 865. While they were competing for MVPs in those years, Howard struck out more than three times as frequently, which showed up

in his batting average—.279 to Pujols' .334.

In isolation MVP voters seem to have no problem lauding Pujols for his defense, his plate discipline, his base-running acumen, and his team leadership. But when it comes time to compare him to a Ryan Howard Type, it comes down to one set of hitting stats against another—and as often as not the voters made the wrong decision anyway.

The Carlos Gonzalez Type or MVP Fatigue: MVP voters love it when a player has finally reached his potential, or blossomed under a new team or manager, or really done anything great after

Cardinal MVPs by Season

Most Valuable Player	Year	Line
Rogers Hornsby	1925#	.403/.489/.756, 39 HR, 143 RBIs
Bob O'Farrell	1926	.293/.371/.433, 7 HR, 68 RBIs
Jim Bottomley	1928	.325/.402/.628, 31 HR, 136 RBIs
Frankie Frisch	1931	.311/.368/.396, 28 SB, 96 R
Dizzy Dean	1934	30–7, 2.66 ERA, 195 SO
Joe Medwick	1937#	.374/.414/.641, 31 HR, 154 RBIs
Mort Cooper	1942	22–7, 1.78 ERA, 152 SO
Stan Musial	1943	.357/.425/.562, 20 3B, 81 RBIs
Marty Marion	1944	.267/.324/.362, .972 Fld%
Stan Musial	1946	.365/.434/.587, 20 3B, 124 R
Stan Musial	1948	.376/.450/.702, 39 HR, 131 RBIs
Ken Boyer	1964	.295/.365/.489, 24 HR, 119 RBIs
Orlando Cepeda	1967	.325/.399/.524, 25 HR, 111 RBIs
Bob Gibson	1968	22–9, 1.12 ERA, 268 SO
Joe Torre	1971	.363/.421/.555, 24 HR, 137 RBIs
Keith Hernandez	1979	.344/.417/.513, 48 2B, 116 R
Willie McGee	1985	.353/.384/.503, 18 3B, 56 SB
Albert Pujols	2005	.330/.430/.609, 41 HR, 117 RBIs
Albert Pujols	2008	.357/.462/.653, 27 HR, 116 RBIs
Albert Pujols	2009	.327/.443/.658, 47 HR, 135 RBIs

Won Triple Crown

having not done anything great before. This is MVP fatigue, a phenomenon that's been around ever since baseball first opened up the award to repeat winners. (In the award's early years, a player was allowed to win it just once, which makes Babe Ruth's single MVP award explicable, if not exactly justifiable.)

By 2006 and 2007 the voters, who reacted so strongly to Ryan Howard and Jimmy Rollins, had already grown tired of Pujols' impossibly consistent excellence. By 2010 he'd hit at least .314 with at least 32 home runs and at least 103 RBIs for 10 consecutive seasons, and even his home run and RBI titles in 2010 weren't enough to wake up voters from their Pujols-induced somnambulism.

So the award went to Joey Votto—himself a borderline Ryan Howard Type—who assembled an outstanding season. Most importantly, Votto had not produced that same outstanding season 10 times before. And Pujols was nearly outvoted by Carlos Gonzalez, who won the batting title but was a long-awaited prospect whose future had been in doubt as recently as 2008.

Everyone likes a great story, and as outstanding a player as Pujols was from 2001 to 2010, his story just lacked suspense. Joey Votto battled anxiety and depression; Carlos Gonzalez overcame a

Remember When...

The only baseball to clear the high, uninterrupted outer walls of Busch Stadium II wasn't a home run at all but the most improbable foul ball in Cardinals history—on September 15, 1986, Mike Laga hit a ball clear out of Busch Stadium, whose arch-patterned façade loomed 130' over the diamond.

questionable understanding of the strike zone; and Ryan Howard just came out of nowhere.

Albert Pujols wasn't novel by the time Barry Bonds had finally left the spotlight; he had already won a batting title and established himself as the best all-around player in baseball before he won his first MVP. He was just consistently, impossibly great and able to do everything on a baseball field with an idiosyncratic, aggressive brilliance.

It's okay to be boring when you're this kind of boring. It's okay to be repetitive if you're being Albert Pujols every year. Pujols won three MVPs in his first decade, but he should have won five, and he could easily have won 10. His hard work and consistency might not endear him to voters looking for a big story, but they made him the symbol of the Cardinals in the 21st century.

Redbird Reference

Ray Lankford

Busch Memorial Stadium, better known as Busch Stadium II, saw Mark McGwire break the single-season home run record and Albert Pujols hit 201 home runs in the first five years of his career. It saw Jim Edmonds launch 40 home runs twice and stood for most of the recent home run era. But none of those fearsome sluggers holds the record for most home runs at Busch II. Instead, the mark will belong forevermore to a center fielder who reached the major leagues primarily because of his speed.

Ray Lankford put on a Cardinals uniform for the first time in 1990, just months after Whitey Herzog left the team in midseason, and at the time Lankford resembled nobody so much as the prototypical Whiteyball outfielder. He was a slick fielder who had stolen more than 100 bases in four years in the minor leagues—to go with 40 triples—but had never hit more than 10 home runs in a season. In 1991, his first full year in the major leagues, he led all of baseball with 15 triples, stole 44 bases, and hit just nine home runs, four of them at Busch.

But something clicked the next year, just before the offensive explosion of 1993—he hit 20 home runs, nearly doubling his professional high. Speed would always be part of his game, but Lankford developed quickly and surprisingly into a patient slugger who was always on base—in spite of some occasionally eye-watering strikeout totals.

Perpetually underrated by fans in and out of St. Louis, Lankford had his two best years in the middle of Mark McGwire mania—in both 1997 and 1998, he hit 31 home runs while getting on base nearly 40 percent of the time, driving in more than 200 total runs and stealing 20 bases each year.

Eventually all those unnoticed home runs added up—Lankford finished with 123 home runs at Busch Stadium, including one as a member of the San Diego Padres. His 2004 comeback as the Cardinals' fourth outfielder allowed him to cap off the record in his final major league at-bat, homering as a pinch-hitter on October 3, 2004. His 228 home runs in a Cardinal uniform rank him fifth all-time.

Unbreakable?

To top Stan Musial's triples record, a Cardinal would have to average nine triples a year for 20 years. The last Cardinal to hit nine triples in a season even *once* was Delino DeShields, who hit 14 in 1997.

Career Batting Leaders

Most Hits

Rank	Player	Hits	Years
1.	Stan Musial	3,630	1941–63
2.	Lou Brock	2,713	1964–79
3.	Rogers Hornsby	2,110	1915–26, 1933
4.	Enos Slaughter	2,064	1938–53
5.	Albert Pujols	2,073	2001–11
6.	Red Schoendienst	1,980	1945–56, 1961–63
7.	Ozzie Smith	1,944	1982–96
8.	Ken Boyer	1,855	1955–65
9.	Curt Flood	1,853	1958–69
10.	Jim Bottomley	1,727	1922–32

Highest Batting Average (minimum 500 games)

Rank	Player	Batting Average	Years
1.	Rogers Hornsby	.359	1915–26, 1933
2.	Tip O'Neill	.344	1884–89, 1891
3.	Johnny Mize	.336	1936–41
4.	Joe Medwick	.335	1932–40, 1947–48
5.	Stan Musial	.331	1941–63
6.	Albert Pujols	.328	2001–11
7.	Chick Hafey	.326	1924–31
8.	Jim Bottomley	.325	1922–32
9.	Frankie Frisch	.312	1927–37
10.	George Watkins	.309	1930–33

Highest On-Base Plus Slugging (OPS) (minimum 500 games)

Rank	Player	OPS	Years
1.	Mark McGwire	1.111	1997–2001
2.	Albert Pujols	1.037	2001–11
3.	Johnny Mize	1.018	1936–41
4.	Rogers Hornsby	.995	1915–26, 1933
5.	Stan Musial	.976	1941–63
6.	Chick Hafey	.948	1924–31
7.	Jim Edmonds	.947	2000–07
8.	Jim Bottomley	.924	1922–32
9.	Joe Medwick	.917	1932–40, 1947–48
10.	Tip O'Neill	.896	1884–89, 1891

Career Batting Leaders

Most Home Runs

Rank	Player	Home Runs	Years
1.	Stan Musial	475	1941–63
2.	Albert Pujols	445	2001–11
3.	Ken Boyer	255	1955–65
4.	Jim Edmonds	241	2000–07
5.	Ray Lankford	228	1990–2001, 2004
6.	Mark McGwire	220	1997–2001
7.	Rogers Hornsby	193	1915–26, 1933
8.	Jim Bottomley	181	1922–32
9.	Ted Simmons	172	1968–80
10.	Johnny Mize	158	1936–41

Most Triples

Rank	Player	Triples	Years
1.	Stan Musial	177	1941–63
2.	Rogers Hornsby	143	1915–26, 1933
3.	Enos Slaughter	135	1938–53
4.	Lou Brock	121	1964–79
5.	Jim Bottomley	119	1922–32
6.	Ed Konetchy	94	1907–13
7.	Willie McGee	83	1982–90, 1996–99
8.	Joe Medwick	81	1932–40, 1947–48
9.	Pepper Martin	75	1928–40, 1944
10.	Tip O'Neill	70	1884–89, 1891

Most Doubles

Rank	Player	Doubles	Years
1.	Stan Musial	725	1941–63
2.	Albert Pujols	455	2001–11
3.	Lou Brock	434	1964–79
4.	Joe Medwick	377	1932–40, 1947–48
5.	Rogers Hornsby	367	1915–26, 1933
6.	Enos Slaughter	366	1938–53
7.	Red Schoendienst	352	1945–56, 1961–63
8.	Jim Bottomley	344	1922–32
9.	Ray Lankford	339	1990–2001, 2004
10.	Ozzie Smith	338	1982–96

Career Batting Leaders

Most Runs Batted In

Rank	Player	Runs Batted In	Years
1.	Stan Musial	1,951	1941–63
2.	Albert Pujols	1,329	2001–11
3.	Enos Slaughter	1,148	1938–53
4.	Jim Bottomley	1,105	1922–32
5.	Rogers Hornsby	1,072	1915–26, 1933
6.	Ken Boyer	1,001	1955–65
7.	Ted Simmons	929	1968–80
8.	Joe Medwick	923	1932–40, 1947–48
9.	Ray Lankford	829	1990–2001, 2004
10.	Lou Brock	814	1964–79

Most Runs Scored

Rank	Player	Runs Scored	Years
1.	Stan Musial	1,949	1941–63
2.	Lou Brock	1,427	1964–79
3.	Albert Pujols	1,291	2001–11
4.	Rogers Hornsby	1,089	1915–26, 1933
5.	Enos Slaughter	1,071	1938–53
6.	Red Schoendienst	1,025	1945–56, 1961–63
7.	Ozzie Smith	991	1982–96
8.	Ken Boyer	988	1955–65
9.	Ray Lankford	928	1990–2001, 2004
10.	Jim Bottomley	921	1922–32

Most Stolen Bases

Rank	Player	Stolen Bases	Years
1.	Lou Brock	888	1964–79
2.	Vince Coleman	549	1985–90
3.	Ozzie Smith	433	1982–96
4.	Arlie Latham	369	1883–89, 1896
5.	Charlie Comiskey	333	1882–89, 1891
6.	Willie McGee	301	1982–90, 1996–99
7.	Tommy McCarthy	270	1888–92
8.	Ray Lankford	250	1990–2001, 2004
9.	Yank Robinson	221	1885–89, 1891
10.	Jack Smith	203	1915–26

Career Batting Leaders

Most Games Played

Rank	Player	Games Played	Years
1.	Stan Musial	3,026	1941–63
2.	Lou Brock	2,289	1964–79
3.	Ozzie Smith	1,990	1982–96
4.	Enos Slaughter	1,820	1938–53
5.	Red Schoendienst	1,795	1945–56, 1961–63
6.	Curt Flood	1,738	1958–69
7.	Albert Pujols	1,705	2001–11
8.	Ken Boyer	1,667	1955–65
9.	Willie McGee	1,661	1982–90, 1996–99
10.	Rogers Hornsby	1,580	1982–96
	Ray Lankford	1,580	1990–2001, 2004

Most Bases on Balls

Rank	Player	Bases on Balls	Years
1.	Stan Musial	1,599	1941–63
2.	Albert Pujols	975	2001–11
3.	Ozzie Smith	876	1982–96
4.	Enos Slaughter	838	1938–53
5.	Ray Lankford	780	1990–2001, 2004
6.	Lou Brock	681	1964–79
7	Rogers Hornsby	660	1915–26, 1933
8.	Jim Edmonds	645	2000–07
9.	Ken Boyer	631	1955–65
10.	Ted Simmons	624	1968–80

Chapter 2

Mark McGwire Breaks the Single-Season Home Run Record

Cardinals' Single-Season Batting Leaders

In 1996, a surprise run to the NLCS got St. Louis excited about baseball again, but it was the 1997 season that truly reignited the city's love affair with its Cardinals. Mark McGwire had just arrived in exchange for three pitching prospects, and he didn't look like anything Cardinals fans had seen before. Whiteyball had been a going concern less than a decade earlier; as recently as 1991 Todd Zeile had led the Cardinals in home runs with 11. McGwire was traded to the Cardinals with 34 already—he finished ninth in the American League that year despite spending the last two months of the season in the National League.

As if waiting for the chance to make the right first impression, McGwire didn't hit any home runs in his first seven games as a Cardinal, all on the road. Then his first homestand came, and newly renovated Busch Stadium was in thrall, for the first time, to the player who would

come to represent the good and the bad of the nineties in baseball. In nine games at Busch McGwire hit five home runs, drove in nine, and slugged .893.

It was September, though, that represented McGwire's real introduction to the National League. In 25 games, McGwire clubbed 15 home runs despite being walked 20 times. No player has ever been so perfectly and single-mindedly designed to hit home runs—for the Cardinals that year he hit 17 singles, just three doubles, and 24 home runs. If a pitch couldn't be driven 450' over the bullpen in right field, he would take it; if he struck out he would get his money's worth, unleashing a swing that made pitchers think twice about taking their eyes off the ball. Eventually fans at Busch learned to set off their flashbulbs with every pitch, just in case.

McGwire's 58 home runs in 1997 were the closest anyone had gotten to Roger Maris' record since George Foster's 52 in 1977, and Ken Griffey Jr., the biggest star in baseball, had come up just short himself with 56. But it was all a prelude to 1998 when McGwire, who unexpectedly signed a contract that would keep him in St. Louis for the rest of his career, promised to do it all over again.

McGwire and Griffey made headlines every morning through the spring, but the chase for 62 home runs didn't become a national

obsession until, on the other end of Interstate 55, the Cubs' Sammy Sosa hit 20 home runs in one month. With one hot month Sosa had vaulted into the home run race and set off the ultimate expression of the Cardinals and Cubs' famous rivalry.

McGwire had started early, homering in the Cardinals' first four games, and by the end of May he had 27 home runs—and not just any home runs, but massive, arcing shots that elicited more gasps than cheers. On May 15, McGwire hit a Livan Hernandez pitch high into center field, hitting the giant *St. Louis Post-Dispatch* sign that marked the farthest part of the second deck from home plate. The home run, so massive that the cameraman aimed too low and missed it entirely, was estimated at the time at 545'; the Cardinals marked the spot with an oversized band-aid.

On the morning of June 1, Griffey was already at 19 and few people outside of Chicago even knew Sosa's name. With just 13 home runs, he trailed not only McGwire and Griffey but veteran sluggers like Juan Gonazalez and Greg Vaughn, not to mention wild cards like Damion Easley. By the end of the month everything had changed, and the home run race shot to the front of every sports page.

Sosa's two home runs on June 1 were followed by a five-game

home run streak; by the time it ended on June 8 he had cracked the MLB top 10, with 20 home runs. It didn't stop there—when the dust settled he'd hit a record 20 home runs in June, tying Griffey at 33 and trailing only McGwire's 37. He'd gained 10 home runs on Big Mac—himself still going at a record pace—in just 27 games.

The home run chase had begun in earnest; newspapers began to run the home run leaders in handy chart form, with McGwire, Sosa, or Griffey a national question and a matter of personal pride. Of course, in Illinois and Missouri, Griffey was not a valid answer—it was Big Mac or Slammin' Sammy, and it would be for the rest of the summer.

After the fireworks of June, July was a let-down—McGwire failed to hit 10 home runs for the first time all year, and Sosa couldn't make up any more ground. Albert Belle hit 16 of his own, but the big three had gotten too much of a head start; Sosa had locked the door behind him.

In August, as Griffey endured a two-week stretch without a home run and fell out of contention for good—he'd finish with 56—McGwire and Sosa roared back to

Redbird Reference

Jesse Burkett

One of the only players in the Cardinals record books able to match Rogers Hornsby hit-for-hit, Jesse Burkett's three-year stint with the Cardinals—then called the St. Louis Perfectos—led directly to the infamously terrible Cleveland Spiders club of 1899.

Earlier that year the Robison brothers, Cleveland businessmen, bought the St. Louis National League club, which had gone bankrupt the year before. Nobody would have complained except they already owned the Spiders, a solid but unspectacular team in their hometown.

Sensing a business opportunity, the brothers transferred Cleveland's best players, including Burkett, Cy Young, and Hall of Fame shortstop Bobby Wallace, to St. Louis. Cleveland, populated now by backups and glorified amateurs, finished an astounding 20–134 and folded the next year.

As for Burkett, who was known as "Crab" in the press and in the dugout for his omnipresent scowl, he hit .378 in three seasons with the Perfectos-turned-Cardinals before jumping to the outlaw American League, where he hit just .290 with the already snake-bitten St. Louis Browns.

life. Sosa briefly took the lead at 48 home runs only to lose it later that day when McGwire clubbed 48 and 49. In the end Sosa's 12 gave him 54 on the year, putting him just one behind Big Mac heading into September.

As Ken Griffey Jr., dropped out, Babe Ruth and Roger Maris stepped in. McGwire was just six home runs away from the record with a full month of baseball left, and he hadn't hit fewer than eight in a month all year. It became clear that both men would break the record—they weren't competing with the ghost of Roger Maris but with each other.

McGwire landed the first punch. Against a Florida Marlins team reeling from the firesale that had followed its World Series victory, McGwire clubbed four home runs in two games to reach 59. On September 5 he became the first player since Maris to hit 60 home runs, launching a home run off future Cardinal Dennys Reyes down Busch Stadium's left field line in the first inning; Sosa homered the same day to reach 58.

After that the Cardinals and Cubs met in Busch Stadium for the last time all season, with McGwire on the brink of history. They'd traded home runs all year; McGwire had hit five of his home runs against the Cubs, while Sosa managed three against the Cardinals. But this time a packed Busch Stadium crowd stood

hushed to see if McGwire could break Roger Maris' record against his biggest rival.

They didn't have long to wait. With two outs in the bottom of the first inning—just minutes removed from Sosa's inning-ending pop-out—McGwire took a 1–1 pitch from journeyman pitcher Mike Morgan and pulled it sharply down the left-field line. It stayed fair and the stadium erupted. The rest of the game, save for each hitter's remaining at-bats—Sosa went 1–5, while McGwire finished 2–4—was anticlimactic.

The next day, with McGwire and Maris tied at 61 and Sosa still lurking, 49,987 fans filled Busch Stadium, each one guarding his ticket stub. The Cubs got to starter Kent Mercker early, going up 2–0 in the first inning, but the Cardinals faithful were only silenced when McGwire grounded out against Steve Trachsel in the bottom of the inning.

Trachsel dispatched the rest of the Cardinals with ease, retiring 10 consecutive batters after allowing a leadoff single to Delino DeShields, so McGwire didn't appear again until the bottom of the fourth inning after Mercker had wormed his way out of a bases-loaded jam in the top to keep it 2–0.

After getting ahead of DeShields and Fernando Tatis and putting them away on 1–2 pitches, Trachsel seemed to be working on autopilot. His first pitch to McGwire was right out of the Steve Trachsel playbook, a knee-high fastball that would have been a called strike to most hitters. McGwire, however, had spent the whole year proving he wasn't most hitters—for all his vaunted patience he couldn't resist bringing his bat through the bottom of the zone in a mighty uppercut.

After a season of impossibly long home runs, number 62 was in doubt until the moment it slipped over the left-field fence and into Busch Stadium's dark inner hallways. In the dugout Tony La Russa, who'd managed McGwire as a rookie, stood fastened to his spot until he saw it clear the fence, staring it all the way over the wall. The crowd was less patient—already on their feet, fans began to scream the moment they saw his famous follow-through. The final estimate was 341', more than 200' shorter than his longest shot of the season.

The game might as well have ended right there. At home plate, mobbed by the rest of the Cardinals, McGwire lifted his uniformed 10-year-old son over his head before getting lost in a sea of white jerseys. As fireworks burst over Busch Stadium he embraced Sosa, who'd witnessed the home run from his perch in right field, and walked to the stands to greet Roger Maris' family, who'd been at the stadium throughout the team's homestand. When play finally resumed Ray Lankford, batting cleanup, struck out swinging on four pitches. It's hard to blame him.

It was a storybook ending to a season that had seemed fated for more than a year, and the Cardinals even won in the end—Lankford hit a three-run home run after McGwire was intentionally walked to break a 2–2 tie. The problem was that it wasn't the ending.

Sosa left St. Louis with 58 home runs, and on September 13 he hit home runs 61 and 62 in an extra-innings comeback against the Milwaukee Brewers. McGwire, just 1–14 since breaking the record, was suddenly tied once more at the top of baseball history. On September 15 McGwire homered to set the new record of 63; on the 16th Sosa tied it. On the 18th

Remember When...

In general, it's a good idea to keep your left-handed relievers from facing the most dominant right-handed hitter baseball has seen in a generation, but three future Cardinal lefty specialists allowed home runs to McGwire in 1998—Dennys Reyes, Ricardo Rincon, and Jason Christiansen. When McGwire became the Cardinals' hitting coach in 2010, Reyes was in the bullpen.

McGwire hit number 64, and on the 20th 65; that record stood until the 23rd, when Sosa hit two more home runs against the Brewers to tie things up again.

On September 25, with just two games left in the season for the Cardinals (compared to three for the Cubs), each man homered to set a new record of 66. (Sosa hit his in the fourth inning, while McGwire couldn't solve the Montreal Expos' pitching staff until the fifth.)

With an extra game on his side, Sosa seemed poised to turn all the ceremony of home run number 62 into trivia. But McGwire had one last home run binge in him. Over the last two games of the season,

while Sosa went 6–13 with all singles, McGwire hit four home runs with his seventh-inning line drive off Carl Pavano giving the Cardinals a lead they wouldn't relinquish and landing the single-season home run record at an incredible 70.

After the last ball had gone over the fence and McGwire had become baseball's first 70-home-run man, he was asked what he thought about the whole season. The typically modest McGwire managed to say he had something in common with the Cardinals fans who'd watched him all summer. "It blows me away," he said. "I'm in awe of myself right now."

Mark McGwire's 1998 Home Run Log

HR	Date	Cardinals Game	McGwire's Game	Opponent, Pitcher	Inning	Sosa HR	Griffey HR
1	3/31	1	1	Los Angeles, Ramon Martinez	5	0	1
2	4/2	2	2	Los Angeles, Frank Lankford	12	0	1
3	4/3	3	3	San Diego, Mark Langston	5	0	2
4	4/4	4	4	San Diego, Don Wengert	6	1	3
5	4/14	13	13	Arizona, Jeff Suppan	3	2	6
6	4/14	13	13	Arizona, Jeff Suppan	5	2	6
7	4/14	13	13	Arizona, Barry Manuel	8	2	6
8	4/17	16	15	Philadelphia, Matt Whiteside	4	3	7
9	4/21	19	18	@ Montreal, Trey Moore	3	3	8
10	4/25	23	21	@ Philadelphia, Jerry Spradlin	7	5	8
11	4/30	27	25	@ Chicago, Marc Pisciotta	8	6	11
12	5/1	28	26	@ Chicago. Rod Beck	9	6	11
13	5/8	34	32	@ New York, Rick Reed	3	7	14
14	5/12	36	34	Milwaukee, Paul Wagner	5	7	15
15	5/14	38	36	Atlanta, Kevin Millwood	4	7	15
16	5/16	40	38	Florida, Livan Hernandez	4	8	15
17	5/18	42	40	Florida, Jesus Sanchez	4	8	16
18	5/19	43	41	@ Philadelphia, Tyler Green	3	8	16
19	5/19	43	41	@ Philadelphia, Tyler Green	5	8	16
20	5/19	43	41	@ Philadelphia, Wayne Gomes	8	8	16
21	5/22	46	43	San Francisco, Mark Gardner	6	9	17

Mark McGwire's 1998 Home Run Log

HR	Date	Cardinals Game	McGwire's Game	Opponent, Pitcher	Inning	Sosa HR	Griffey HR
22	5/23	47	44	San Francisco, Rich Rodriguez	4	9	17
23	5/23	47	44	San Francisco, John Johnstone	5	9	17
24	5/24	48	45	San Francisco, Robb Nen	12	9	18
25	5/25	49	46	Colorado, John Thomson	1	11	18
26	5/29	52	49	San Diego, Dan Miceli	9	13	18
27	5/30	53	50	San Diego, Andy Ashby	1	13	18
28	6/5	59	53	San Francisco, Orel Hershiser	1	17	22
29	6/8	62	56	Chicago (AL), Jason Bere	4	20	24
30	6/10	64	58	Chicago (AL), Jim Parque	3	20	25
31	6/12	65	59	Arizona, Andy Benes	3	20	26
32	6/17	69	63	Houston, Jose Lima	3	25	26
33	6/18	70	64	Houston, Shane Reynolds	5	25	27
34	6/24	77	71	Cleveland, Jaret Wright	4	31	30
35	6/25	78	72	Cleveland, Dave Burba	1	32	30
36	6/27	79	73	Minnesota, Mike Trombley	7	32	31
37	6/30	81	75	Kansas City, Glendon Rusch	7	33	33
38	7/11	89	83	Houston, Billy Wagner	11	35	37
39	7/12	90	94	Houston, Sean Bergman	1	35	37
40	7/12	90	94	Houston, Scott Elarton	7	35	37
41	7/17	95	89	Los Angeles, Brian Bohanon	1	36	39
42	7/17	95	89	Los Angeles, Antonio Osuna	8	36	39
43	7/20	98	92	San Diego, Brian Boehringer	5	36	39
44	7/26	104	98	@ Colorado, John Thomson	4	38	40
45	7/28	105	99	Milwaukee, Mike Myers	8	41	40
46	8/8	115	108	Chicago, Mark Clark	4	44	41
47	8/11	118	111	New York, Bobby Jones	4	46	41
48	8/19	124	117	@ Chicago, Mark Karchner	8	48	42
49	8/19	124	117	@ Chicago, Terry Mulholland	10	48	42
50	8/20	125	118	@ New York, Willie Blair	7	48	43
51	8/20	126	119	@ New York, Rick Reed	1	48	43
52	8/22	130	123	@ Pittsburgh, Francisco Cordova	1	49	44
53	8/23	131	124	@ Pittsburgh, Ricardo Rincon	8	51	44
54	8/26	133	125	Florida, Justin Speier	8	52	44
55	8/30	137	129	Atlanta, Dennis Martinez	7	54	47
56	9/1	139	131	@ Florida, Livan Hernandez	7	55	47
57	9/1	139	131	@ Florida, Donn Pall	9	55	47
58	9/2	140	132	@ Florida, Brian Edmondson	7	56	47
59	9/2	140	132	@ Florida, Rob Stanifer	8	56	47
60	9/5	142	134	Cincinnati, Dennys Reyes	1	58	48
61	9/7	144	136	Chicago, Mike Morgan	1	58	50
62	9/8	145	137	Chicago, Steve Trachsel	4	58	50
63	9/15	152	144	Pittsburgh, Jason Christiansen	9	62	52
64	9/18	155	147	@ Milwaukee, Rafael Roque	4	63	53
65	9/20	157	149	@ Milwaukee, Scott Karl	1	63	53
66	9/25	161	153	Montreal, Shayne Bennett	5	66	56
67	9/26	162	154	Montreal, Dustin Hermanson	4	66	56
68	9/26	162	154	Montreal, Kirk Bullinger	7	66	56
69	9/27	163	155	Montreal, Mike Thurman	3	66	56
70	9/27	163	155	Montreal, Carl Pavano	7	66	56

Single-Season Batting Leaders

Most Home Runs in a Single Season

Rank	Player	Home Runs	Year
1.	Mark McGwire	70	1998
2.	Mark McGwire	65	1999
3.	Albert Pujols	49	2006
4.	Albert Pujols	47	2009
5.	Albert Pujols	46	2004
6.	Albert Pujols	43	2003
	Johnny Mize		1940
8.	Albert Pujols	42	2010
	Jim Edmonds		2004
	Jim Edmonds		2000
	Rogers Hornbsy		1922

Most Triples in a Single Season

Rank	Player	Triples	Year
1.	Perry Werden	29	1893
2.	Tom Long	25	1915
	Roger Connor		1894
4.	Stan Musial	20	1946
	Stan Musial		1943
	Jim Bottomley		1928
	Rogers Hornsby		1920
	Duff Cooley		1895
9.	Tip O'Neill	19	1887
	Garry Templeton		1979

Most Doubles in a Single Season

Rank	Player	Doubles	Year
1.	Joe Medwick	64	1936
2.	Joe Medwick	56	1937
3.	Stan Musial	53	1953
4.	Tip O'Neill	52	1887
	Enos Slaughter		1939
6.	Albert Pujols	51	2004
	Albert Pujols		2003
	Stan Musial		1944
9.	Stan Musial	50	1946
10.	Scott Rolen	49	2003

Single-Season Batting Leaders

Most Hits in a Single Season

Rank	Player	Hits	Year
1.	Rogers Hornsby	250	1922
2.	Joe Mewick	237	1937
3.	Rogers Hornsby	235	1921
4.	Joe Torre	230	1971
	Stan Musial		1948
6.	Stan Musial	228	1946
7.	Jim Bottomley	227	1925
	Rogers Hornsby		1924
9.	Jesse Burkett	226	1901
10.	Tip O'Neill	225	1887

Singles in a Single Season

Rank	Player	Singles	Year
1.	Jesse Burkett	185	1899
2.	Jesse Burkett	181	1901
3.	Curt Flood	178	1964
4.	Milt Stock	170	1920
	Jesse Burkett		1900
6.	Joe Torre	164	1971
7.	Willie McGee	162	1985
8.	Curt Flood	160	1968
	Red Schoendienst		1949
10.	Lou Brock	159	1974

Extra-Base Hits in a Single Season

Rank	Player	XBH	Year
1.	Stan Musial	103	1948
2.	Rogers Hornsby	102	1922
3.	Albert Pujols	99	2004
4.	Joe Medwick	97	1937
5.	Albert Pujols	95	2003
	Joe Medwick		1936
7.	Albert Pujols	93	2009
	Jim Bottomley		1928
9.	Stan Musial	92	1953
10.	Mark McGwire	91	1998

Single-Season Batting Leaders

Single-Season Batting Average

Rank	Player	Batting Average	Year
1.	Tip O'Neill	.435	1887
2.	Rogers Hornsby	.424	1924
3.	Rogers Hornsby	.403	1925
4.	Rogers Hornsby	.401	1922
5.	Rogers Hornsby	.397	1921
6.	Jesse Burkett	.396	1899
7.	Rogers Hornsby	.384	1923
8.	Jesse Burkett	.376	1901
9.	Stan Musial	.376	1948
10.	Joe Medwick	.374	1937

Single-Season On-Base Percentage

Rank	Player	OBP	Year
1.	Rogers Hornsby	.507	1924
2.	John McGraw	.505	1900
3.	Tip O'Neill	.490	1887
4.	Rogers Hornsby	.489	1925
5.	Mark McGwire	.483	2000
6.	Mark McGwire	.470	1998
7.	Jesse Burkett	.463	1899
	Bob Caruthers		1887
9.	Albert Pujols	.462	2008
10.	Rogers Hornsby	.459	1923
	Rogers Hornsby		1923
	Rogers Hornsby		1922

Single-Season Slugging Percentage

Rank	Player	SLG	Year
1.	Rogers Hornsby	.756	1925
2.	Mark McGwire	.752	1998
3.	Mark McGwire	.746	2000
4.	Rogers Hornsby	.722	1922
5.	Stan Musial	.702	1948
6.	Mark McGwire	.697	1999
7.	Rogers Hornsby	.696	1924
8.	Tip O'Neill	.691	1887
9.	Albert Pujols	.671	2006
10.	Albert Pujols	.667	2003

Single-Season Batting Leaders

Runs Scored in a Single Season

Rank	Player	Runs	Year
1.	Tip O'Neill	167	1887
2.	Arlie Latham	163	1887
3.	Arlie Latham	152	1886
4.	Jesse Burkett	142	1901
5.	Rogers Hornsby	141	1922
6.	Charlie Comiskey	139	1887
7.	Albert Pujols	137	2003
	Tommy McCarthy		1890
9.	Tommy McCarthy	136	1889
10.	Stan Musial	135	1948
	Bill Gleason		1887

Runs Batted In in a Single Season

Rank	Player	RBI	Years
1.	Joe Medwick	154	1937
2.	Rogers Hornsby	152	1922
3.	Mark McGwire	147	1999
	Mark McGwire		1998
5.	Rogers Hornsby	143	1925
6.	Joe Medwick	138	1936
7.	Albert Pujols	137	2006
	Joe Torre		1971
	Johnny Mize		1940
	Jim Bottomley		1929

Bases on Balls in a Single Season

Rank	Player	Bases on Balls	Year
1.	Mark McGwire	162	1998
2.	Jack Clark	136	1987
	Jack Crooks		1892
4.	Mark McGwire	133	1999
5.	Jack Crooks	121	1893
6.	Yank Robinson	118	1889
7.	Dummy Hoy	117	1891
8.	Miller Huggins	116	1910
	Yank Robinson		1888
10.	Albert Pujols	115	2009

Single-Season Batting Leaders

Stolen Bases in a Single Season

Rank	Player	Stolen Bases	Year
1.	Arlie Latham	129	1887
2.	Lou Brock	118	1974
3.	Charlie Comiskey	117	1887
4.	Vince Coleman	110	1985
5.	Vince Coleman	109	1987
	Arlie Latham		1888
7.	Vince Coleman	107	1986
8.	Tommy McCarthy	93	1888
9.	Curt Welch	89	1887
10.	Tommy McCarthy	83	1890

Intentional Bases on Balls in a Single Season

Rank	Player	Intentional BB	Year
1.	Albert Pujols	44	2009
2.	Albert Pujols	38	2010
3.	Albert Pujols	34	2008
4.	Albert Pujols	28	2006
	Mark McGwire		1998
6.	Albert Pujols	27	2005
7.	Stan Musial	26	1958
8.	Ted Simmons	25	1977
9.	Orlando Cepeda	23	1967
10.	Albert Pujols	22	2007
	Ted Simmons		1979

Times Hit by Pitch in a Single Season

Rank	Player	Times Hit By Pitch	Year
1.	Steve Evans	31	1910
2.	Chief Roseman	29	1890
3.	Fernando Vina	28	2000
4.	Dan McGann	24	1900
5.	Dan McGann	23	1901
	John McGraw		1900
7.	Fernando Vina	22	2001
	Dick Harley		1898
9.	Solly Hemus	20	1952
10.	Steve Evans	19	1911

Single-Season Batting Leaders

Strikeouts in a Single Season

Rank	Player	Strikeouts	Year
1.	Jim Edmonds	167	2000
2.	Ron Gant	162	1997
3.	Mark McGwire	155	1998
4.	Ray Lankford	151	1998
5.	Jim Edmonds	150	2004
6.	Colby Rasmus	148	2010
	Ray Lankford		2000
8.	Ray Lankford	147	1992
9.	Ryan Ludwick	146	1911
10.	Mark McGwire	141	1999

Sacrifice Flies in a Single Season

Rank	Player	Sacrifice Flies	Year
1.	George Hendrick	14	1982
2.	Tom Herr	13	1985
3.	Pedro Guerrero	12	1989
	Tom Herr		1987
	Keith Hernandez		1982
6.	Pedro Guerrero	11	1990
	George Hendrick		1983
	Ray Jablonski		1954
9.	Edgar Renteria	10	2004
	Jim Edmonds		2001
	Ozzie Smith		1990
	Ted Simmons		1971

Single-Season Batting Leaders by Position

Pitcher

Category	Number	Player	Year
Home Runs	5	Bob Gibson	1972, 1965
Runs Batted In	21	Dizzy Dean	1935
Batting Average	.381	Curt Davis	1939

Catcher

Category	Number	Player	Year
Home Runs	26	Ted Simmons	1979
Runs Batted In	103	Ted Simmons	1974
Batting Average	.332	Ted Simmons	1975

Single-Season Batting Leaders by Position

First Base

Category	Number	Player	Year
Home Runs	70	Mark McGwire	1998
Runs Batted In	147	Mark McGwire	1998, 1999
Batting Average	.371	Jim Bottomley	1923

Second Base

Category	Number	Player	Year
Home Runs	42	Rogers Hornsby	1922
Runs Batted In	152	Rogers Hornsby	1922
Batting Average	.424	Rogers Hornsby	1924

Third Base

Category	Number	Player	Year
Home Runs	34	Scott Rolen	2004
Runs Batted In	137	Joe Torre	1971
Batting Average	.363	Joe Torre	1971

Shortstop

Category	Number	Player	Year
Home Runs	16	Edgar Renteria	2000
Runs Batted In	100	Edgar Renteria	2003
Batting Average	.330	Edgar Renteria	2003

Left Field

Category	Number	Player	Year
Home Runs	34	Albert Pujols	2002
Runs Batted In	154	Joe Medwick	1937
Batting Average	.435	Tip O'Neill	1887

Center Field

Category	Number	Player	Year
Home Runs	42	Jim Edmonds	2004
Runs Batted In	111	Jim Edmonds	2004
Batting Average	.353	Willie McGee	1985

Right Field

Category	Number	Player	Year
Home Runs	37	Ryan Ludwick	2008
Runs Batted In	130	Enos Slaughter	1946
Batting Average	.357	Stan Musial	1943

CHAPTER 3

STAN THE MAN HITS FIVE HOME RUNS IN A DOUBLEHEADER
Cardinals' Single-Game Records and Achievements

Today Stan Musial is St. Louis' private treasure, a brilliant outfielder so underrated by the baseball public at large that he had to be added to Major League Baseball's All-Century Team by a special committee after the voters chose 10 other outfielders ahead of him. Around Busch Stadium he's ubiquitous— he holds most of the Cardinals records worth holding, appears on most of the lists he doesn't lead, and stands permanently at the ready in the form of two different statues on the stadium grounds.

He was, as the pedestal of the larger statue has informed generations of Cardinals fans who never saw him play, "baseball's perfect warrior... baseball's perfect knight," a player who did nothing to discredit his team and a man who did nothing to discredit the game of baseball. And perfection is somehow easier to forget than the more flawed brilliance of his contemporaries.

Given how frequently he's forgotten today, though, it's sometimes too easy to forget just how much he terrorized other teams whose fans didn't have the privilege of forgetting about him while he was busy lacing one of his 177 triples or 725 doubles into the gaps of every National League park he visited. Even his nickname, so much a part of his identity that nobody in town will ask who you're talking about when you're talking about The Man, came from somewhere else; Brooklyn fans tired of watching him circle the diamond game after game were said by various sources to have groaned something to the effect of, "Here comes that man again!"

Redbird Reference
Johnny Mize

Perennially overlooked, it took another first baseman emerging fully formed as an MVP candidate to bring the original Big Cat back into the St. Louis limelight. After Albert Pujols started his incredible run, Cardinals fans searching for historical analog found that few players anticipated Pujols quite like their own Johnny Mize.

A big, nimble first baseman with an incredible batting eye, Mize arrived in the Major Leagues in 1936 and hit .329 with 19 home runs and 93 RBIs, finishing third in the National League with an OPS of .979. There was no learning curve for Big Jawn; from 1937 to 1941 he won a batting title, led the league in home runs and RBIs twice and OPS three times, and finished within the Top 10 in MVP voting four times.

Like Pujols, he was an aggressive hitter who couldn't be struck out. With the Cardinals he walked 424 times while notching just 279 strikeouts. In 1939 and 1940 he won two legs of the Triple Crown, finishing third in RBIs in 1939 and fifth in batting average in 1940.

In 1941 he was abruptly traded by Branch Rickey, who was reluctant to pay Mize's high salary and constantly preoccupied with trading players before their skills declined. Mize's skills, to say the least, had not. In 1942, now a New York Giant, he hit 26 home runs and drove in a league-leading 110 before spending three full seasons in the Navy during World War II.

Returning to the Giants in 1946, Mize hit 22 home runs in 101 games before putting together one of his most impressive seasons in 1947. That year he hit 51 home runs while striking out just 42 times, a feat unmatched in the history of baseball. After another MVP-caliber season, Mize spent the remainder of his career as the New York Yankees' pinch-hitting specialist, retiring after 1953 at 40.

Contemporary Comparo: I'll give you three guesses. Hint: He's mentioned in this sidebar.

Cardinals Single-Game Achievements and Records and In-Season Home Run Feats

Individual Single Game Records

Record	Number	Player	Opponent	Date
At-Bats	10	Fernando Vina	Florida Marlins	4/27/2003
Hits	6	Last accomplished by Skip Schumaker	New York Mets	7/26/2008
Singles	6	Skip Schumaker	New York Mets	7/26/2008
Doubles	4	Joe Medwick	Boston Braves	8/4/1937
Triples	3	Les Bell	Brooklyn Dodgers	9/22/1926
		Jim Bottomley	Boston Braves	5/15/1923
Home Runs	4	Mark Whiten	Cincinnati Reds	9/7/1993
Grand Slams	2	Fernando Tatis	Los Angeles Dodgers	4/23/1999
Total Bases	16	Mark Whiten	Cincinnati Reds	9/7/1993
RBI	12	Mark Whiten	Cincinnati Reds	9/7/1993
		Jim Bottomley	Brooklyn Dodgers	9/16/1924
RBIs in an Inning	8	Fernando Tatis	Los Angeles Dodgers	4/23/1999
Sacrifice Flies	3	Vince Coleman	San Diego Padres	5/1/1986
Runs	5	Ten times, last accomplished by J.D. Drew	Montreal Expos	5/1/1999
Bases on Balls	5	Four times, last accomplished by Colby Rasmus	Kansas City Royals	5/22/2011
Strikeouts	5	Six times, last accomplished by Ray Lankford	Chicago Cubs	8/8/1998
Double Plays	3	Three times, last accomplished by Albert Pujols	San Diego Padres	3/31/1911
Stolen Bases	5	Lonnie Smith	San Francisco Giants	9/4/1982

That man—The Man—was an equal-opportunity groan-inducer, but his exploits in New York have proven especially unforgettable. The most impressive day of his career came against a team a borough away from his frustrated Brooklyn admirers, in Manhattan. On May 2, 1954, Stan The Man hit five home runs in a doubleheader against the New York Giants, who would eventually run away with the National League and the World Series.

Game 1 saw the Cardinals lined up against the Giants' young staff ace, Johnny Antonelli, who would go on to finish 21–7 with an ERA of 2.30, and St. Louis had him on the run in a hurry. After a leadoff home run from Wally Moon, Red Schoendienst scored on a two-out base hit to make it 2–0. Musial's first plate appearance ended with a walk, and he was erased on a fielder's choice by the next batter. That was the only time the Giants would retire him in Game One.

Musial homered in the third to make it 3–0 Cardinals, but the Giants roared back in the fourth inning, tying the ballgame on back-to-back doubles from Hank Thompson and Monte Irvin. The Cardinals got out of that jam when Willie Mays was erased on a double play, but back-to-back home runs in the fifth inning put the Giants up 5–4.

That's when Stan Musial

Redbird Reference

Mark Whiten

"Hard Hittin'" Mark Whiten was never a star player, but fans who watched him patrol the outfield in person during the Cardinals' lean years of the early 1990s would be forgiven for making that mistake. Whiten couldn't hit for average and rapped suspiciously few doubles for a would-be power hitter, but the things he *could* do stuck with you; nobody had a better throwing arm in right field, and he could make things happen with his surprising speed on the bases.

And the Hard Hittin', of course—he did that, too. On September 7, 1993, 31,231 fans at Cincinnati's Riverfront Stadium got the chance to watch Whiten pulverize Reds pitching for four home runs and a major league record-tying 12 RBIs in support of Bob Tewksbury. Whiten remains the only Cardinal—and one of 15 players ever—to hit four home runs in a single game.

Whiten reached starter Larry Luebbers early, tagging him for a grand slam in the first inning of the game, but the Reds starter was the only pitcher who managed to get Whiten out that afternoon, retiring him on a foul ball to third base in the fourth inning. From there, Whiten ruined the day of reliever Mike Anderson, slamming a three-run shot after Anderson walked the first two batters he faced and hitting his third home run of the day with two more runners on in the seventh inning. (Anderson was somehow left in to face one more batter after that drubbing—Tom Pagnozzi singled to chase him from the game.)

With the score already 12–2, the Reds brought in damaged closer Rob Dibble to mop up. Soon to go down permanently with arm problems, Dibble put together one of his best performances on the season, striking out five batters in two innings of work. Unfortunately, none of those batters was Mark Whiten who, with Gerald Perry on in front of him for the fourth time, hit Dibble's best out of the park for his fourth homer and his 12th RBI.

stopped having a good game and started having a historic game. In the bottom of the fifth, after Red Schoendienst scrambled to first base on an error, Musial homered to put the Cardinals up 6–5; that lasted until the top of the next inning when the Giants tied things up again on Irvin's home run.

After a single in the sixth inning, Musial came up in the eighth inning with Giants swingman Jim Hearn on the mound and the game in his hands. Wally Moon and Red Schoendienst were already on base when there went that man again—Musial hit a long home run, his third of the game and his sixth of the young season, to put the Cardinals on top for good.

In Game 2 the Cardinals took a mortal blow from the Giants in the fourth inning when Leo Durocher's offense came to life and scored eight runs off two different Cardinals pitchers. Down 8–3, and with Hall of Fame reliever Hoyt Wilhelm in to close out the game, Musial got to work immediately, opening the fifth inning with a

Remember When...

Fernando Viña's game-winning base hit on April 27, 2003, came in his 10th at-bat in the 20th inning—after he'd gone 0–9.

two-run homer deep to right field to cut the score to 8–6. In the seventh inning Musial touched Wilhelm again, hitting another home run to the same spot and bringing the Cardinals within one, but that's as close as they would get. The Giants brought in another run in the ninth inning, and the Cardinals lost 9–7.

That Giants team would go on to win the World Series; Musial ended the season with a .330 batting average, 35 home runs, and 126 RBIs. For most players that would be a career season, but it was only the fifth-highest OPS of his career. For most players five home runs in a doubleheader would be a defining moment. But like most other things Stan Musial did in his career, it's been lost in the sheer volume of Hall of Fame moments

Unbreakable?

Only two players in the 150-year history of Major League Baseball, Mark Whiten and Jim Bottomley, have ever driven in 12 runs in a game—and both of them were Cardinals, almost 70 years apart.

Behind the Numbers

A player hits for the cycle when he collects a single, a double, a triple, and a home run in the same game. The Cardinals have had a player hit for the cycle 19 times since 1887.

Cardinals Hitting for the Cycle

Player	Opponent	Date
Tip O'Neill	Cleveland	4/30/1887
Tip O'Neill	Louisville	5/7/1887
Tommy Dowd	Louisville	8/16/1895
Cliff Heathcote	@ Philadelphia	6/13/1918
Jim Bottomley	@ Philadelphia	7/15/1927
Chick Hafey	Philadelphia	8/21/1930
Pepper Martin	@ Philadelphia	5/25/1933
Joe Medwick	@ Cincinnati	6/29/1935
Johnny Mize	New York (NL)	7/13/1940
Stan Musial	@ Brooklyn	7/24/1949
Bill White	@ Pittsburgh	8/14/1960
Ken Boyer	Chicago (NL)	9/14/1961
Ken Boyer	@ Houston	6/16/1964
Joe Torre	@ Pittsburgh	6/27/1973
Lou Brock	San Diego	5/27/1975
Willie McGee	@ Chicago (NL)	6/23/1984
Ray Lankford	New York (NL)	9/15/1991
John Mabry	@ Colorado	5/18/1996
Mark Grudzielanek	Milwaukee	4/27/2005

30 Home Run Seasons

Player	Home Runs	Season	Player	Home Runs	Season
Mark McGwire	70	1998	Jack Clark	35	1987
Mark McGwire	65	1999	Stan Musial		1954
Albert Pujols	49	2006	Ripper Collins		1934
Albert Pujols	47	2009	Scott Rolen	34	2004
Albert Pujols	46	2004	Albert Pujols		2002
Albert Pujols	43	2003	Fernando Tatis		1999
Johnny Mize		1940	Dick Allen		1970
Albert Pujols	42	2010	Stan Musial	33	1955
Jim Edmonds		2004	Albert Pujols	32	2007
Jim Edmonds		2000	Mark McGwire		2000
Rogers Hornsby		1922	Ken Boyer		1960
Albert Pujols	41	2005	Stan Musial		1951
Jim Edmonds	39	2003	Ray Lankford	31	1998
Stan Musial		1948	Ray Lankford		1997
Rogers Hornsby		1925	Joe Medwick		1937
Ryan Ludwick	37	2008	Jim Bottomley		1928
Albert Pujols		2008	Lance Berkman		2011
Albert Pujols		2001	Jim Edmonds		2001
Albert Pujols		2011	Ron Gant		1996
Stan Musial	36	1649	Stan Musial		1953

he collected in 22 years as the player who defined what it meant to be a Cardinal.

The full measure of Musial's achievement can't be seen from close up—it's when you back up and view the Cardinals' entire record book that you get the picture. He's the Cardinals' all-time leader in games played by nearly five full seasons, in triples by thirty, in doubles by nearly 300, in runs scored and runs batted in by more than 500, and in hits by nearly a thousand. In his 22 years with the Cardinals, he was on base more than 5,000 times.

But what Stan Musial means to his team, his city, and his sport can never quite be captured by what he achieved. Nobody else managed to hit five home runs in a doubleheader until Nate Colbert, the lone star of the hapless expansion-era San Diego Padres, managed the feat in 1972. A St. Louis native, Colbert mentioned later that he'd been in the stands for Musial's five-homer day back in 1954 when he was eight years old.

That's what Stan Musial means to the St. Louis Cardinals, and to St. Louis Cardinals fans, and even to those endlessly disenchanted Brooklyn Dodgers rooters that gave him his nickname. If you forget why people play baseball, or how baseball is supposed to be played, Stan Musial is the ultimate reminder—baseball's perfect warrior, baseball's perfect knight.

Remember When...

Albert Pujols' 30-game hitting streak began on July 12, 2003, when he went 3–5 with a home run, but the next game only the vagaries of Major League Baseball's hitting streak rules kept the non-streak alive—after being hit by a pitch in his first plate appearance, Pujols was ejected in the ensuing brawl, leaving him without an at-bat.

That's how Pujols came into the third game of his historic run with a one-game hitting streak on the line.

Unbreakable?

Albert Pujols' five grand slams in 2009 tied him with Ernie Banks for the National League's single-season record.

Behind the Numbers

Rogers Hornsby holds the St. Louis Cardinals' record for longest hitting streak, but he doesn't have the St. Louis record—the Browns put together three longer streaks before leaving for Baltimore in 1953. George Sisler had hitting streaks of 41 and 35 games in 1922 and 1924–25, while George McQuinn had a 34-game hitting streak in 1938.

Hornsby still holds the record for longest St. Louis hitting streak by a man who wasn't named George.

Unbreakable?

Tip O'Neill, on his way to a .435 batting average for the St. Louis Brown Stockings, hit for the cycle on consecutive Saturdays in the spring of 1887. O'Neill is one of three players ever to hit for the cycle twice in the same year.

Remember When...

On May 18, 1996, John Mabry hit for the "Natural Cycle" when he hit a single, a double, a triple, and a home run in order at Coors Field. It was the first natural cycle for the Cardinals since Ken Boyer did it in 1964, and the 11th natural cycle in major league history. Mabry hit just six triples in a major league career that lasted 14 seasons.

Grand-Slam Home Runs in a Single Season

Rank	Player	Grand Slams	Year
1.	Albert Pujols	5	2009
2.	Jim Bottomley	3	1925
	Keith Hernandez		1977
	Fernando Tatis		1999
3.	28 times	2	2010

Cardinals Hitting Streaks

Player	Games	Season
Rogers Hornsby	33	1922
Stan Musial	30	1950
Albert Pujols	30	2003
Harry Walker	29	1943
Ken Boyer		1959
Curt Flood		1961–62
Joe Medwick	28	1935
Red Schoendienst		1954
Lou Brock	26	1971
Joe McEwing	25	1999

Grand-Slam Home Runs in a Career

Rank	Player	Grand Slams	Years
1.	Albert Pujols	12	2001–11
2.	Stan Musial	9	1941–63
3.	Rogers Hornsby	7	1915–26, 1933
	Ken Boyer		1955–65
	Ted Simmons		1968–80
6.	Jim Bottomley	6	1922–32
	Bill White		1959–65, 1969
8.	Ron Northey	5	1947–49
	Tim McCarver		1959–69, 1973–74
	Keith Hernandez		1974–83
	Ray Lankford		1990–2001, 2004
	Mark McGwire		1997–2001
	Fernando Tatis		1998–2000
	Jim Edmonds		2000–07

Three Home Run Games in Cardinals History (Since 1919)

Player	Opponent	Date
George Harper	@ New York Giants	9/20/1928
George Watkins	@ Philadelphia	6/24/1931
Johnny Mize	Boston	7/13/1938
	New York	7/20/1938
	@ Cincinnati	5/13/1940
	Pittsburgh	9/8/1940
Stan Musial	New York Giants	5/2/1954
	@ New York Mets	7/8/1962
Bill White	@ Los Angeles	7/5/1961
Reggie Smith	@ Philadelphia	5/22/1976
Mark McGwire	Arizona	4/14/1998
	@ Philadelphia	5/19/1998
	@ Philadelphia	5/18/2000
Albert Pujols	@ Chicago	7/20/2004
	Cincinnati	4/16/2006
	Pittsburgh	9/3/2006
	@ Chicago	5/30/2010

Players Who Homered in Their First At-Bat

Player	Date
Eddie Morgan#	4/14/1936
Wally Moon	4/13/1954
Keith McDonald	7/4/2000
Chris Richard#	7/17/2000
Gene Stechschulte#	4/17/2001
Hector Luna	4/8/2004
Adam Wainwright#	5/24/2006
Mark Worrell	6/5/2008

Homered on first pitch of first at-bat.

Remember When...

Keith McDonald is one of two players in Major League Baseball history to hit a home run in his first two at-bats. McDonald, who would hit just three home runs in his major league career, hit a home run as a pinch hitter on July 4, 2000, then hit a home run in the first at-bat of his only career start on July 6.

The three home runs are the only hits of his major league career.

Remember When...

On April 23, 1999, Fernando Tatis became the only player in baseball history to hit two grand slams in a single inning when he took Chan Ho Park out of Dodger Stadium twice in the Cardinals' 11–5 victory. Tatis would later hit two grand slams in a season twice more, in 2000 and again as a reserve outfielder for the New York Mets in 2009.

Remember When...

Three of the last four Cardinals to hit home runs in their first at-bat—and the last two to do it on the first pitch—were pitchers. Mark Worrell's homer in 2008 came with two runners on base.

CHAPTER 4

LOU BROCK BREAKS EVERY LAST STOLEN BASE RECORD
Cardinals' Postseason Batting Records

When Lou Brock reached the major leagues for the first time, in 1961, Maury Wills led the National League in stolen bases with 35. Two years before that, in 1959, Luis Aparicio had stolen 56 bases, the first time anyone had topped 50 since 1943.

Each new barrier—30 stolen bases, 40, 50—was as improbable as the last, for less than a decade earlier that kind of baserunning had been a lost art. With home runs plentiful following World War II, the stolen base had gone abruptly and effectively extinct by the 1950s. In 1950, Dom DiMaggio had led the American League with 15; in 1956, the first of nine consecutive seasons where he led the AL, Aparicio had done it with 21.

While Brock was getting his feet wet with the Cubs—he wouldn't steal any bases in his four 1961 appearances—the Cardinals were getting their feet cast in lead. Julian Javier led the team in stolen bases that year with 11; Bill White, who led the team in attempts, stole just eight bases in 19 tries.

No Cardinal had stolen 30 bases in a season since Frankie Frisch in 1927, 12 years before Lou Brock was born. In the meantime, entire teams of Redbirds had stopped running. In 1951 Solly Hemus and Enos Slaughter led the Cardinals with seven each; the year before, Tommy Glaviano and Stan Musial were the only Cardinals to swipe five. Players led St. Louis in stolen bases occasionally by speed and mostly by accident.

Things changed across the league in 1962 when Wills abruptly showed baseball what it had been missing. That year, after a relatively sedate start, the Dodgers shortstop had stolen 19 bases in May and 15 more in June. With 46 stolen bases at the All-Star Break—he'd been caught stealing just five times—he finally inaugurated the new era of base-thievery, stealing 31 in September to reach 104 for the season.

It was the first time since 1900 that anyone had stolen 100 bases in a season, and it exposed a generation of catchers who hadn't had to deal with that kind of threat before. In the meantime, Brock had stolen 16 bases for the Cubs—a nice bonus, but not as impressive as the 23-year-old's seven triples or nine home runs. In 1963 he swiped 24 more to finish sixth in the National League, but his 12 times

Redbird Reference

Gregg Jefferies

Gregg Jefferies is most famous today as a can't-miss prospect who was pushed too far and too fast by the Mets. But for one perfect season with the Cardinals, he became one of the strangest stars in baseball history.

In 1987, at the height of the rivalry that saw Cardinals fans brand the Mets pond scum, Jefferies was the best prospect in baseball. That year, as a 19-year-old already in AA ball, he hit .367 with 48 doubles, 20 home runs, and 101 RBIs to go along with 26 stolen bases. Few scouts had ever seen such a broad-based skillset, but mismanagement by the Mets and distrusting veterans meant he was exiled to the Midwest before he turned 24.

Try to find another player answering to the description Jefferies fit in 1993 when he emerged from five disappointing seasons to make the NL All-Star Team and earn MVP votes for a struggling Cardinals team. That year he was a first baseman who hit .342 with average power—16 home runs—and stole 46 bases. Perhaps most impressively, he walked 62 times while notching just 32 strikeouts in 544 at-bats.

He was nearly as brilliant at the plate the next year, hitting .325 with 12 home runs in strike-shortened 1994, but the bizarre speed was gone and the Cardinals decided against building on their unlikely star. Allowed to leave as a free agent in the offseason, Jefferies put together six more middling seasons before retiring. But his breakout 1993 remains one of the most unique All-Star years in Cardinals history.

Lou Brock's World Series Record

Year	G	AB	R	H	2B	3B	HR	RBI	SB	BB	SO	AVG	OBP	SLG
1964	7	30	2	9	2	0	1	5	0	0	3	.300	.300	.467
1967	7	29	8	12	2	1	1	3	7	2	3	.414	.452	.655
1968	7	28	6	13	3	1	2	5	7	3	4	.464	.516	.857
Career	21	87	16	34	7	2	4	13	14	5	10	.391	.424	.655

Career Postseason Hits

Rank	Player	Batting Average	Hits
1.	Albert Pujols	.330	88
2.	Jim Edmonds	.277	61
3.	Yadier Molina	.309	54
4.	Willie McGee	.284	48
5.	Lou Brock	.391	34
	Ozzie Smith	.236	
7.	Edgar Renteria	.250	32
8.	Tom Herr	.221	31
	Fernando Vina	.333	31
10.	Scott Rolen	.228	26

Career Postseason Home Runs

Rank	Player	Slugging Percentage	Home Runs
1.	Albert Pujols	.607	18
2.	Jim Edmonds	.523	13
3.	Larry Walker	.526	6
4.	Scott Rolen	.421	5
	David Freese	.794	
6.	Willie McGee	.426	4
	Lou Brock	.655	
8.	Mike Shannon	.370	3
	Ron Gant	.600	
	J.D. Drew	.453	
	Reggie Sanders	.378	

caught stealing had left him fourth in that dubious category.

Brock's speed was certainly an important part of his game when the Cardinals pulled the trigger on the infamous trade that sent Ernie Broglio to the Cubs. But on June 15, 1964, Brock had just 10 stolen bases in 52 games for the Cubs. At the time Cardinals fans could have been just as excited about his .361 average with the Class-C St. Cloud Rox before his rookie season or his burgeoning home run power.

Brock's baserunning, it turned out, was a sight to behold, but his effect on the Cardinals' faltering pennant chances was even more impressive. On the day of the trade, the Cardinals stood at 28–31 after a 9–3 loss in empty Colt Stadium; arriving in Houston the next day and batting second behind Curt Flood, Brock reached base four times, tripled, scored a run, and stole a base.

With Brock's bat in the lineup—he would hit .348 with the Cardinals that year, with 12 home runs and nine triples—the Cardinals' sputtering offense seemed to click. The team hit .283 and went 65–38 in its last 103 games, storming out of the basement to stun the Phillies and win one of the most improbable pennants in National League history, and Brock seemed to get better as the months went on.

In September and October, when the Cardinals went 22–10 and secured the pennant on the last day of the season, Brock hit .364 with six home runs, scoring an incredible 30 runs and driving in 17 more. That performance helped

Redbird Reference
Tommy Herr

Old Hollywood lore has it that you could tell how much moviegoers liked two famous Jameses—Stewart and Cagney—by how invariably their names were shortened to Jimmy in everyday conversation. All through the 1980s, the Cardinals' second baseman was dutifully reported on baseball cards as Tom Herr, but the moment he stepped onto the Busch Stadium Astroturf he became Tommy, Ozzie Smith's impossibly competent keystone partner for three National League pennants.

Herr didn't run like the other Whiteyball stalwarts, and with Ozzie Smith on his right he wasn't about to impress the Cardinals faithful with any defensive acrobatics. With those two avenues to stardom closed off, he seemed to respond by doing nearly everything well. A solid defender with a great eye and occasional doubles power, Herr spent 13 major league seasons honing a skillset that only impressed fans when they realized he didn't do anything unimpressive.

That skillset was perfected in 1985 when Herr hit .302 with 38 doubles, 31 stolen bases, 80 walks, and—incredibly, given his eight home runs—110 RBIs. Herr remains the last National League player to drive in at least 100 runs with fewer than 10 home runs, and it's no wonder—that kind of thing is only possible when you're doing everything else right.

secure the Cardinals' first National League pennant since 1946, and it made Lou Brock a St. Louis icon.

That summer, after showing only flashes with Chicago, Lou Brock the toolsy young outfielder also became Lou Brock the preternatural stolen-base threat. By July 1 he had 17, but it was that August that he gave St. Louis fans a preview of what was to come, stealing 14 bases in 28 games. He finished the year with 43, just 10 behind Wills for the National League lead.

Brock wouldn't play Maury Wills' understudy much longer; starting in 1966 Brock would lead the National league eight times in the next nine seasons. For 12 years running, Brock would steal at least 51 bases, but it was 1974 before the 35-year-old would finally begin his rewrite of the record books.

Like Wills before him, Brock's season started off typically enough. In April he stole 13 bases and was caught just once; in May he snagged 17 in 18 tries. Maybe that early success emboldened him for what was to come, because after taking an incredible 60 at the All-Star Break—no one else in the National League finished the season with more than 59—he began running even more. On September 1 Brock stood at 94 stolen bases after taking 29 in 29 August starts.

By then nobody should've doubted that he would threaten

Behind the Numbers

No statistic in baseball is quite so victim to expansion as postseason statistics—of the players on this list, only Lou Brock earned all his hits prior to the addition of the League Championship Series in 1969; Albert Pujols, Jim Edmonds, Yadier Molina, Edgar Renteria, Fernando Vina, and Scott Rolen acquired all their hits after the introduction of the Wild Card in 1995.

Wills' modern record of 104, but the four bases he stole on September 1 convinced any stragglers. That month Brock reached base safely 48 times and stole 24 bases, stealing his 105th by September 10 and running the record out to 118 on September 29 when he took his last base of the season against none other than the Chicago Cubs.

With the single-season record in hand, Brock and Brock-watchers turned their eyes to the modern career record, which had belonged to Ty Cobb since 1928. Brock, who hadn't begun running in earnest until he was 25, seemed like a poor bet to threaten the career mark; by his own age-25 season, Cobb had led the league in stolen bases three times, and stolen more than 400 in his career.

But Brock's relentless pace and his incredible durability brought

Redbird Reference

Larry Walker

The 2004 Cardinals were already 69–38—nearly 10 games ahead of the pack in the National League Central—when they surprised all of baseball by trading for Larry Walker in early August. It almost seemed unfair; the Cardinals already had the MV3 trio of Albert Pujols, Jim Edmonds, and Scott Rolen, who were each having career years. Walker transformed them from a great offense into an impossibly great offense.

At 37 years old, Walker had missed most of the season with various career-threatening injuries before the Rockies activated him and set about trading him to a playoff contender for his final act, but he looked perfectly healthy in the Cardinals' stretch run, hitting .280 with 11 home runs and even four stolen bases in 44 games on the way to 105 regular-season wins.

But both Walker and the Cardinals had made the trade for the postseason—and Walker didn't disappoint in his first October action since 1995. He finished that season's World Series run with six home runs and 11 RBIs. Even against Boston, when the Cardinals' bats abruptly stopped working, Walker hit .357 with two doubles and two home runs in the sweep.

him closer to the Georgia Peach every year, and his 118 stolen bases at 35—when Cobb had finally begun slowing down—cut the deficit from 171 steals, as it had been when both men were 34, to just 62. At 753, Brock was just 144 bags away from the career record.

As it turned out, he didn't have another 100-steal season left in his 36-year-old legs, and he'd never lead the league again. But during the next two years—by which time Ernie Broglio had been retired for 10 years—Brock grabbed another 112 bases.

Suddenly he was just a season's work away from Ty Cobb's record—but that 1977 season would be one of the toughest of Brock's career. Now 38 and the elder statesmen on a team filled with young stars like Ted Simmons, Keith Hernandez, and Garry Templeton, Brock fell apart in the summer after a solid start.

From Opening Day he wasn't his usual dangerous self on the basepaths, and in June his bat started to fail. He hit .241 that month and entered July with just 12 stolen bases in 22 attempts. Now only a few steals away, Brock endured one of the worst months of his career; in July he added six stolen bases, albeit in 10 attempts, but hit just .188. In August 29, looking like a player on the way out, he stole his 893rd base, setting what was recognized as the new all-time record. (Ty Cobb's career stolen base total was later revised up from 892 to 897.)

But his record chase had been built on consistency and durability, and Lou Brock, as it turned out, had something left in the tank after all. In September his bat came back all at once. When he became the first player to steal 900 bases in the live-ball era, against the New York Mets, he did it in style, going 2–4, driving in a run, and stealing numbers 899 and 900 in a 7–2 Cardinals win.

Unbreakable?

In 2011 Albert Pujols became just the third player ever to hit three home runs in a single World Series game, and the first to do it for the National League. Pujols' five hits and six RBIs that night were also career postseason highs.

Lou Brock would retire two years later with 938 stolen bases, 3023 hits, and a host of appearances in the Cardinals' record book. Only Stan Musial had played more than his 2,289 games with the team or scored more than his 1,427 runs, and when Brock retired, his 888 Cardinals stolen bases put him 685 ahead of Jack Smith, who

Redbird Reference
David Eckstein

It's difficult to look less like a baseball player than David Eckstein did, whether you're a baseball player or not. Listed at a generous 5'6"—2" shorter than Ross Barnes, the National League's first batting champion and a dainty middle infielder even for 1876—Eckstein seemed to slap down at the ball when he swung and, to get the baseball from shortstop to first base, ran into a full-body hurl so violent that it seemed amazing that he stayed upright after every 6–3 putout.

However he did it, Eckstein parlayed a keen batter's eye, an incredible work ethic, and a willingness to take a baseball in the ribs into a crucial role on two separate World Series champions. The two-time All-Star had already picked up nine World Series hits for the 2002 Anaheim Angels when he keyed the Cardinals' improbable 2006 victory, going 8–22 with three doubles and four RBIs.

ranked second in team history since 1901.

Brock's regular season career left a permanent mark on the records, but his World Series career left three pennants and two championships in old Busch Stadium's rafters. Brock hit the ground running in his first season with the Cardinals, hitting .300 and driving in five runs, including a Game 7 home run in Bob Gibson's gutsy victory over the Yankees.

In 1967 Brock was even better, batting .414 and scoring eight of the team's 25 runs in a seven-game victory over the Red Sox. Even in 1968, when he made the ultimately fatal decision to run home standing up instead of sliding in a crucial Game 5 loss to the Tigers, Brock was outstanding;

he hit .464 with a triple and two home runs and stole seven bases. His 13 hits are tied for the most ever in a single World Series.

But his legacy didn't end with his playing career. Brock's relentless style of play anticipated the Whiteyball Cardinals of the 1980s, who got on base, put their heads down, and sprinted like a team full of Lou Brocks. After Brock became the first player in team history to do it, three more Cardinals stole more than 300 bases in the 1980s, and Vince Coleman, perhaps the best pure basestealer in baseball history, stole 100 bases three years in a row between 1985 and 1987. Lou Brock had popularized a new weapon on offense, and for 10 years after he retired, that weapon defined an entire organization.

Career Postseason RBI

Rank	Player	RBI
1.	Albert Pujols	52
2.	Jim Edmonds	41
3.	Yadier Molina	23
4.	Willie McGee	22
5.	David Freese	21
6.	Tom Herr	15
7.	Edgar Renteria	13
	Reggie Sanders	
	Lou Brock	
10.	David Eckstein	12
	Larry Walker	

Cardinals World Series MVPs

1964	Bob Gibson
1967	Bob Gibson
1982	Darrell Porter
2006	David Eckstein
2011	David Freese

Cardinals NLCS MVPs

1982	Darell Porter
1985	Ozzie Smith
2004	Albert Pujols
2006	Jeff Suppan
2011	David Freese

CHAPTER 5

JOE MEDWICK WINS THE LAST NATIONAL LEAGUE TRIPLE CROWN

Cardinals Batting Champions and Triple Crown Contenders

"Ducky" Joe Medwick started hitting the moment he reached the major leagues, and for a solid decade the Cardinals' star outfielder never stopped. Just 20 years old when he was plucked from Branch Rickey's nascent farm system in 1932, Medwick hit .349 in 26 games and immediately showed off the aggressive, powerful swing that would put him in the center of the Cardinals' batting order. In 106 at-bats, Medwick hit 12 doubles while walking only twice.

Fans learned quickly that Joe Medwick didn't get cheated. He didn't walk much, and at first he struck out frequently, but in an era of slap-happier hitters, few players did more when they put the ball in play than he did. In 1934 Medwick, who struck out 83 times and led baseball with 18 triples, hit .369 and slugged .610 when he didn't swing and miss. The balls he hit were stung— just 22, he finished third in baseball with 76 extra-base hits.

In one of the highest-scoring eras in baseball history, Medwick's particular brand of slugging still made him something of an odd Ducky Wucky (he preferred to be called "Muscles" but had to settle, eventually, for his hated nickname being

shortened to Ducky). The home run had already been established as the primary weapon in a team's offensive arsenal, but Medwick at his best was an incomparable doubles hitter, lacing line drives and running until the outfield could make him stop.

In 1934 that earned him the wrong kind of recognition; his uncompromising baserunning, and his general uncompromisingness, got him thrown out of Tiger Stadium in the seventh game of the 1934 World Series. With Dizzy Dean backed up by seven runs and already cruising to a shutout victory, Medwick laced an extra-base hit off the right-field wall, scoring Pepper Martin from second. Unsatisfied with a double and an eight-run lead, Medwick

Redbird Reference

Jim Bottomley

"Sunny" Jim Bottomley won two legs of the Triple Crown and the MVP Award in 1928 when he led the St. Louis Cardinals to the National League pennant. Suddenly the offensive star of the Cardinals with Rogers Hornsby gone, Bottomley led the league in home runs, RBIs, and triples to drive an offense that finished second in the NL in runs scored.

The season perfectly encapsulated the cheerful first baseman's career. A line-drive hitter who loved to hit the ball into the gaps and run, that year he became the second player in Major League Baseball history to hit 20 doubles, 20 triples, and 20 home runs in the same season. He's also one of two players—both Cardinals—to drive in 12 runs in a single game, a feat he accomplished in 1924.

He might hold the most historical importance, however, as the first MVP product of Branch Rickey's farm system, an innovation that would change baseball forever and turn the Cardinals of the 1930s into perennial pennant contenders.

Bottomley was also one of several Cardinals stars to return to the city and play for the American League Browns in his twilight years, and probably the most successful. In 1936 Bottomley went to play for the bottom-dwelling Browns and hit .298 with 11 triples, 12 home runs, and 95 RBIs. The next year, fittingly enough, he would replace fellow ex-Cardinal Rogers Hornsby as player-manager.

Contemporary Comparo: A well-rounded slugger who could compete for the MVP at his best, Bottomley looks a little like Mark Teixeira, if you squint, with a pinch of Sean Casey's happiest-man-in-baseball reputation.

made the turn for third base and slid in safely for a triple, just in time to get spiked by Detroit Tigers third baseman Marvin Owen.

Medwick, who could also be driven to violence by transgressions other than calling him "Ducky Wucky," took a moment to collect himself and then kicked Owen square in the stomach with his own spikes. The benches cleared, but things cooled off after Ripper Collins drove in Medwick (and away from Owen), and the inning appeared to end without incident moments later.

That was when the riot began. When Medwick took his place in left field for the bottom of the sixth, Detroit's fans showered him first with boos and then with fruit—"Mostly apples, oranges, and grapefruits," reported biographer Charles Faber, but also bottles. Rather than cowering, the Gashouse Gang lived up to its playful reputation by tossing the fruit around the horn, the fans grew even more furious and the field grew so cluttered with produce and trash that the umpires had to stop play.

Behind the Numbers

Rogers Hornsby became the only National Leaguer ever to win the major league Triple Crown in 1925.

Remember When

In 1990 Willie McGee managed to win the National League batting championship despite being traded to the American League Oakland Athletics in midseason! McGee hit just .274 in Oakland, but Eddie Murray—whose .330 batting average led the major leagues—was unable to catch up to McGee's stationary target.

This circus repeated itself three times—Tiger Stadium personnel clearing the field, Medwick attempting to return to his position, the fans pelting the outfielder with foodstuffs and non-perishables—until Judge Kenesaw Mountain Landis, baseball's dour commissioner, called Owens and Medwick to his seats, the game having been delayed nearly 20 minutes already.

Up to this point Medwick had remained in the game, but when he made the mistake of telling Landis he didn't have any reason for kicking Owens except, "Well, you know a lot of things happen when you slide into third," the commissioner quickly sorted things out. Medwick was removed from the game and the grounds under police escort and the Cardinals, with Chick Fullis in left and the apples, oranges, and grapefruits on ice, rolled on to an 11–0 victory.

Redbird Reference

Rogers Hornsby

While Ty Cobb and then Babe Ruth were dominating the American League, creating larger-than-life personalities and leaving their marks on the record books and the public's perception of baseball, Rogers Hornsby just hit.

Playing for a Cardinals team that found itself perennially out of pennant contention, "The Rajah" began his career as the best hitter at the twilight of the Deadball Era and in 1922 made one of the National League's smoothest transitions into the home run age, hitting a major league–leading 42 while driving his batting average to new heights.

But following 1926, after Hornsby's down season coincided with the Cardinals' first World Series championship, he was gone and few seemed to miss him. That was Rogers Hornsby in his own time: undeniably brilliant, but never popular.

Like Ty Cobb, his American League nemesis, a particularly sympathetic observer might have called Hornsby the baseball player intense; a less-understanding one might settle for surly. Hornsby played the game because it was all he liked to do—he told *Sport* magazine that it didn't make any difference where he went or what the result was, "So long as I can play the full nine." Lee Allen, the baseball historian, called him "frank to the point of being cruel and as subtle as a belch," and Hornsby probably wouldn't have disagreed.

He didn't read the newspaper and he didn't like newspapers because he worried about his eyesight. All he enjoyed was baseball and gambling on the horses, and losing at one usually led to more of the other.

But behind all that gruffness and single-mindedness was a combination of talent and hustle that led him to become the greatest hitter the National League had ever seen. Nothing seemed to phase Hornsby—he hit through unpopularity, bad teams, new teams, and the most dramatic strategy change in baseball history. Before Babe Ruth showed what the home run was capable of and inaugurated the live-ball era, Hornsby used his impressive speed to turn line-drives into triples. After that twice led the league in home runs. Hornsby managed to lead the league in slugging percentage with marks of both .484 in 1917 and .756 in 1925 before and after everything changed.

From 1921 to 1925, while the Cardinals around him failed again and again to get their acts together, Hornsby put together one of the most dominant runs in the history of baseball, hitting .402 and twice winning the Triple Crown.

After he left the Cardinals, Hornsby bounced from team to team, then league to league, and eventually job to job, always hitting and never quite belonging. But maybe it wasn't only about his surliness and his gruffness—in the end, Hornsby's famous quote about the offseason might say all that needs to be said about his career. He didn't do funny things that sportswriters could tell us about; he didn't do things we could relate to, as fans, or act as our moral compass, or anything else. "People ask me what I do in winter when there's no baseball," he's supposed to have said. "I'll tell you what I do. I stare out the window and wait for spring."

What would he do, the fans must have wondered, if he just didn't strike out so much? Medwick wasn't much for ceremony—it took him all of one season to show them. In 1935 he cut his strikeouts by more than a third and hit .353 as a result, leading the league in total bases for the first of three consecutive seasons. His 64 doubles in 1936 are still the single-season National League record, and over the course of his career he averaged an incredible 44 per 162 games.

By 1937 his batting average was perennially among the league leaders, and his free-swinging nature and extra-base hits made him a constant threat to lead the league in RBIs—he had the year before with 138. But a Triple Crown watcher would have been forgiven for dismissing the Cardinal outfielder as a threat because he'd never finished higher than fourth in the National League home run race—and it had never been a close one, at that. In 1935 he'd hit a career high 23 home runs, which only tied him with Ripper Collins for the team lead and left him 11 behind Boston's Wally Berger. In 1936 he'd fallen to 18, 15 behind perennial league leader Mel Ott.

Medwick simply wasn't a home run hitter—he'd led the league in hits and doubles and managed nearly 100 extra-base hits, but Mel Ott had, by then, hit 30 home runs or more three years running.

Medwick would only top 30 home runs—or even 25—once in his career, but everything seemed to go his way in 1937. On May 1 he was hitting .441. On June 1 he had fallen all the way to .410, but he'd tallied nine home runs and 38 RBIs to go along with his usual 14 doubles. As late as August 19 Muscles—he was probably able to make his teammates call him Muscles that year—was hitting

.400 to go along with 26 home runs and 120 RBIs.

By then, with a month and a half left in the season, Medwick had already wrapped up the two jewels of the Triple Crown he'd been expected to contest. His nearest competition for the batting title was teammate Johnny Mize, who was hitting .364, and no other National Leaguer that season would finish with even 116 RBIs.

But Mel Ott, whose ferocious swing had been tuned perfectly to the New York Giants' famously odd ballpark, was just two home runs away, at 24, and a hitting binge to start the final month of the season gave him 31 by September 14. By then Medwick had begun to fall off, if only by his own lofty standards; his batting average was down to .375, he'd only added 18 RBIs to his league-leading total, and he was down by three home runs with three weeks to go.

Just then, a funny thing happened: Mel Ott stopped hitting home runs. Despite a schedule that saw his Giants play 15 of

Redbird Reference

Arlie Latham

Arlie Latham, who began his career with the St. Louis Browns of the American Association before floating around baseball until 1909, was nicknamed "The Freshest Man on Earth" for several reasons. (He was also called "The Dude," if you like that sort of thing.) Here are three of them:

1. Latham sometimes put on a clown nose when walking behind the Browns' eccentric owner, Chris von der Ahe.
2. Latham's antics cost the Browns the pennant on the final day of the season in 1889 when, by way of suggesting the umpire call the game on account of darkness with the Browns in the lead, he lit 12 large candles on the Browns' bench.
3. As the Browns' ersatz third-base coach, Latham particularly enjoyed running up and down the baseline shouting insults during the opposing pitcher's delivery. This led directly to the introduction of the coach's boxes beside each base.

This list could go on almost indefinitely, but the publishers insist we save that for *The Freshest Cardinals Record Book On Earth*.

Contemporary Comparo: Maybe a self-aware Rickey Henderson with Brian Wilson's beard?

National League Triple Crown Winners

Year	Player	AVG	HR	RBI
1887	Tip O'Neill	.435#	14	123
1922	Rogers Hornsby	.401	42#	152
1925	Rogers Hornsby	.403#	39#	143#
1937	Joe Medwick	.374#	31	154

#: Led Major League Baseball

their last 19 games at the Polo Grounds, where he would hit nearly two-thirds of his 511 career home runs, Ott didn't hit a single homer over the last three weeks of the season, batting an empty .300 instead; 1937 became one of the few seasons in which Ott would hit more home runs on the road (16) than at home.

Meanwhile, Medwick continued to swing hard and often. He'd walk just twice in his last 20 games, hitting .369 and driving in 16 runs to bring his total to a career-high 154. And on September 29, with four games to go, Medwick hit his 31st home run of the season to take his share of the league lead.

It was a strangely anticlimactic home run race after promising such a wild finish, but somehow Medwick had done it—he'd tied Mel Ott for the home run lead while maintaining his comfortable lead in batting average and his enormous RBI cushion. With both players slumping quietly to the finish line, Medwick became the sixth Triple Crown winner in

National League history. Hitting .374, he'd clubbed 31 home runs and driven in a team-record 154 runs.

Cardinals fans in 1937 couldn't have understood the gravity of the situation immediately; Rogers Hornsby had won two Triple Crowns in four years a little more

Behind the Numbers

Count Campau's home run title is interesting for at least one reason: It came in his second and final major league season.

In 1890 a failed attempt to unionize led many of the best players in the National League and the American Association to bolt for a bootstrapped Players' League. Campau, who had washed out of the National League after a lackluster performance in 1888, hit .322 and drove in 75 runs in the vastly weakened AA—he even managed the Browns for 42 games that year—but couldn't find a job in 1891, when the Players' League folded.

Redbird Reference

Vince Coleman

Everyone on the Whiteyball Cardinals of the 1980s could run, but Vince Coleman might have been the best pure basestealer in the history of baseball. A tenth-round pick in 1982, Coleman arrived at rookie-level Johnson City that June and immediately began running—that year he stole 43 bases in 46 attempts in just 58 games. In 1983 he stole an astonishing 145 bases in 113 games with low A Macon.

In 1985 he was promoted to the major leagues where he didn't appear to be phased—he stole 110 bases that year to lead the National League for the first of six consecutive seasons. In 1986 he hit just .232, and that might be the most impressive of his seasons for sheer determination—despite earning just 168 total bases in 154 games, Coleman stole 107 stolen bases and was caught only 14 times.

The Cardinals of the 1980s played Whiteyball; at his best, Vince Coleman, getting on base with a walk or a single and then immediately turning it into a double, *was* Whiteyball.

---

than a decade earlier, and Lou Gehrig had won the last American League Triple Crown in 1934. Ted Williams would win two more in 1942 and 1947.

But for all the players who would come close in the years to follow, Joe Medwick's down-to-the-wire win remains the most recent Triple Crown in the National League. Whether anyone had realized it at the time, Medwick had made the kind of history that only looms larger with each passing year.

So would Medwick. Notoriously brusque with reporters, Ducky Joe had to wait 20 years before they would finally elect him to the Hall

of Fame, in 1968. When asked about what it felt like to stay on the ballot so long, he likened it to something he hadn't dealt with often as a player: "It was like a 20-year slump."

Medwick's Triple Crown was fitting in a way—with it Cardinals have won three of the National League's six Triple Crowns, and the four they've won as a franchise remains a major league record. Along with Hornsby's two, including a rare major league Triple Crown, Medwick is joined in that rarefied group by Tip O'Neill, who hit .435 for the American Association's St. Louis Browns in 1887.

Cardinals Batting Champions

Year	Player	AVG	Year	Player	AVG
1887†	Tip O'Neill	.435	1946	Stan Musial	.365
1888†	Tip O'Neill	.335	1948	Stan Musial	.376
1901	Jesse Burkett	.376	1950	Stan Musial	.346
1920	Rogers Hornsby	.370	1951	Stan Musial	.355
1921	Rogers Hornsby	.397	1952	Stan Musial	.336
1922	Rogers Hornsby	.401	1957	Stan Musial	.351
1923	Rogers Hornsby	.384	1971	Joe Torre	.363
1924	Rogers Hornsby	.424	1979	Keith Hernandez	.344
1925	Rogers Hornsby	.403	1985	Willie McGee	.353
1931	Chick Hafey	.349	1990	Willie McGee	.335
1937	Joe Medwick	.374	2003	Albert Pujols	.359
1939	Johnny Mize	.349			
1943	Stan Musial	.357			

†: Tip O'Neill's two batting championships were earned in the American Association.

Cardinals Hits Leaders

Year	Player	Hits	Year	Player	Hits
1887†	Tip O'Neill	225	1943	Stan Musial	220
1888†	Tip O'Neill	177	1944	Stan Musial	197
1901	Jesse Burkett	226	1946	Stan Musial	228
1920	Rogers Hornsby	218	1948	Stan Musial	230
1921	Rogers Hornsby	235	1949	Stan Musial	207
1922	Rogers Hornsby	250	1952	Stan Musial	194
1924	Rogers Hornsby	227	1964	Curt Flood	211
1925	Jim Bottomley	227	1979	Garry Templeton	211
1936	Joe Medwick	223	1985	Willie McGee	216
1937	Joe Medwick	237	2003	Albert Pujols	212
1942	Enos Slaughter	188			

Cardinals Home Run Champions

Year	Player	Runs	Year	Player	Runs
1882†	Oscar Walker	7	1937	Joe Medwick	37
1887†	Tip O'Neill	14	1939	Johnny Mize	28
1890†	Count Campau	9	1940	Johnny Mize	43
1922	Rogers Hornsby	42	1998	Mark McGwire	70
1925	Rogers Hornsby	39	1999	Mark McGwire	65
1928	Jim Bottomley	31	2009	Albert Pujols	47
1934	Ripper Collins	35	2010	Albert Pujols	42

Cardinals Doubles Leaders

Year	Player	Doubles	Year	Player	Doubles
1887†	Tip O'Neill	52	1943	Stan Musial	48
1911	Ed Konetchy	38	1944	Stan Musial	51
1920	Rogers Hornsby	44	1946	Stan Musial	50
1921	Rogers Hornsby	44	1948	Stan Musial	46
1922	Rogers Hornsby	46	1949	Stan Musial	41
1924	Rogers Hornsby	43	1950	Red Schoendienst	43
1925	Jim Bottomley	44	1952	Stan Musial	42
1926	Jim Bottomley	40	1953	Stan Musial	53
1931	Sparky Adams	46	1954	Stan Musial	41
1936	Joe Medwick	64	1963	Dick Groat	43
1937	Joe Medwick	56	1968	Lou Brock	46
1938	Joe Medwick	47	1979	Keith Hernandez	48
1939	Enos Slaughter	52	1989	Pedro Guerrero	42
1941	Johnny Mize	39	2003	Albert Pujols	51
1942	Marty Marion	38			

Cardinals Triples Leaders

Year	Player	Triples	Year	Player	Triples
1887†	Tip O'Neill	19	1949	Stan Musial	13
1893	Perry Werden	29		Enos Slaughter	
1915	Tom Long	25	1951	Stan Musial	12
1917	Rogers Hornsby	17	1966	Tim McCarver	13
1921	Rogers Hornsby	18	1968	Lou Brock	14
1928	Jim Bottomley	20	1977	Garry Templeton	18
1934	Joe Medwick	18	1978	Garry Templeton	13
1938	Johnny Mize	16	1979	Garry Templeton	19
1942	Enos Slaughter	17	1985	Willie McGee	18
1943	Stan Musial	20	1991	Ray Lankford	15
1946	Stan Musial	20	1997	Delino DeShields	14
1948	Stan Musial	18			

Cardinals RBI Champions

Year	Player	RBIs	Year	Player	RBIs
1886†	Tip O'Neill	107	1940	Johnny Mize	137
1887†	Tip O'Neill	123	1942	Johnny Mize	110
1920	Rogers Hornsby	94	1946	Enos Slaughter	130
1921	Rogers Hornsby	126	1948	Stan Musial	131
1922	Rogers Hornsby	152	1956	Stan Musial	109
1925	Rogers Hornsby	143	1964	Ken Boyer	119
1926	Jim Bottomley	120	1967	Orlando Cepeda	111
1928	Jim Bottomley	138	1971	Joe Torre	137
1936	Joe Medwick	138	1999	Mark McGwire	147
1937	Joe Medwick	154	2010	Albert Pujols	118
1938	Joe Medwick	122			

Cardinals Runs Scored Leaders

Year	Player	Runs Scored	Year	Player	Runs Scored
1886†	Arlie Latham	152	1954	Stan Musial	120
1887†	Tip O'Neill	167	1967	Lou Brock	113
1901	Jesse Burkett	142	1971	Lou Brock	126
1921	Rogers Hornsby	131	1979	Keith Hernandez	116
1922	Rogers Hornsby	141	1980	Keith Hernandez	111
1924	Rogers Hornsby	121	1982	Lonnie Smith	120
1933	Pepper Martin	122	2003	Albert Pujols	137
1937	Joe Medwick	111	2004	Albert Pujols	133
1946	Stan Musial	124	2005	Albert Pujols	129
1948	Stan Musial	135	2009	Albert Pujols	124
1951	Stan Musial	124	2010	Albert Pujols	115
1952	Stan Musial	105			
	Solly Hemus				

Cardinals Stolen Base Leaders

Year	Player	Stolen Bases	Year	Player	Stolen Bases
1888†	Arlie Latham	109	1969	Lou Brock	53
1890†	Tommy McCarthy	83	1971	Lou Brock	64
1900	Patsy Donovan	45	1972	Lou Brock	63
1927	Frankie Frisch	48	1973	Lou Brock	70
1931	Frankie Frisch	28	1974	Lou Brock	118
1933	Pepper Martin	26	1985	Vince Coleman	110
1934	Pepper Martin	23	1986	Vince Coleman	107
1936	Pepper Martin	23	1987	Vince Coleman	109
1945	Red Schoendienst	26	1988	Vince Coleman	81
1966	Lou Brock	74	1989	Vince Coleman	65
1967	Lou Brock	52	1990	Vince Coleman	77
1968	Lou Brock	62			

CHAPTER 6

BOB GIBSON FINISHES WITH A 1.12 ERA IN THE YEAR OF THE PITCHER

Cardinals' Single-Season Starting Pitching Records

In history as in life, Bob Gibson is difficult to grasp. His career is defined by a few contradictory threads—his sterling career and one unimaginable season, his consistent work all summer, and his ability to reach an even higher level in the World Series—that come together to draw a full picture of the best pitcher in Cardinals history.

But if Bob Gibson must be summarized in a sentence, or a number, a couple come to mind immediately: 1968; 1.12. The Year of the Pitcher. In that infamous year before the mound was lowered and hitters were allowed back into the game, Bob Gibson was The Pitcher, setting the

modern ERA record and looking as unhittable as any starter ever has.

The story starts in 1967. After a disappointing regular season—he had finished just 13–7 in 24 starts with an ERA of 2.98 after a line drive from Roberto Clemente broke his right fibula—Gibby almost single-handedly won the Cardinals the World Series in 1967, going 3–0 with an ERA of 1.00 across three consecutive complete games and, while he was at it, hitting a home run.

It was the kind of heroic performance the Cardinals had come to expect from Gibson, who'd emerged as the staff ace in 1962 after solving the control problems that had caused him to walk 119 batters a year before. Between 1963 and 1966 he'd averaged 20 wins a season to go along with 236 strikeouts and 10 hit batsmen, and in 1964

Behind the Numbers

Game Score is a formula designed by Bill James to estimate just how effective a pitcher was in a particular start. Ernie Broglio's 97 ties him for the 39th best nine-inning start since the beginning of the live ball era; Roy Parmelee's 17-inning win, in which he allowed one run and struck out nine, puts him in a tie for fifth best extra-inning start.

he'd played a crucial role in the Cardinals' first World Series championship since 1946, winning Game 5 and coming back on short rest to win Game 7. He'd already been an All-Star three times, won two Gold Gloves, pitched 25 shutouts, and received MVP votes twice.

For all that accomplishment, though, and for all the fear his blistering fastball and sharp breaker had instilled in National League hitters, he'd never made a case for himself as the best pitcher in baseball. It took a year dominated by pitchers to show that he was better than any of them, and a summer in which he was almost literally unhittable, to make it clear to baseball at large.

The first sign that things would be different in 1968 might have come in May, when Gibson went into extra innings on consecutive starts to earn wins—on May 1 he pitched 12 innings and allowed no earned runs to disappoint the Astrodome faithful, and back home against the Mets on May 6 it took the Cardinals 11 innings to get the second run they'd need to earn Gibson his third win of the season.

But that run support problem would be a recurring theme. Gibson lost his next four starts despite allowing just seven earned runs over 33 innings! On May 17, in Philadelphia, he threw a nine-inning shutout only to *lose the game* in the 10th, when former

Bob Gibson's 1968 Game-By-Game Performance

Date	Opponent	Score	IP	H	R	ER	BB	SO	W–L	ERA
4/10	Atlanta	2–1	7.0	3	1	0	1	0	ND	0.00
4/15	@Atlanta	4–3	7.0	5	3	3	3	5	ND	1.93
4/20	Chicago	1–5	9.0	10	5	3	1	8	0–1	2.35
4/26	Pittsburgh	2–1	9.0	7	1	1	1	5	1–1	1.97
5/1	@Houston	3–1	12.0	7	1	0	5	7	2–1	1.43
5/6	New York	2–1	11.0	3	1	1	1	11	3–1	1.31
5/12	Houston	2–3	8.0	11	3	2	2	10	3–2	1.43
5/17	@Philadelphia	0–1	9.2	7	1	1	4	5	3–3	1.36
5/22	Los Angeles	0–2	8.0	1	1	1	2	6	3–4	1.34
5/28	San Francisco	1–3	8.0	4	3	3	1	5	3–5	1.52
6/2	@New York	6–3	9.0	7	3	3	3	8	4–5	1.66
6/6	@Houston	4–0	9.0	3	0	0	2	5	5–5	1.52
6/11	@Atlanta	6–0	9.0	5	0	0	2	4	6–5	1.40
6/15	Cincinnati	2–0	9.0	4	0	0	0	13	7–5	1.30
6/20	Chicago	1–0	9.0	5	0	0	1	6	8–5	1.21
6/26	Pittsburgh	3–0	9.0	4	0	0	0	7	9–5	1.14
7/1	@Los Angeles	5–1	9.0	9	1	1	2	4	10–5	1.13
7/6	@San Francisco	3–0	9.0	6	0	0	4	9	11–5	1.06
7/12	Houston	8–1	9.0	3	1	1	0	8	12–5	1.06
7/21	New York	2–0	9.0	7	0	0	0	13	13–5	1.01
7/25	Philadelphia	5–0	9.0	5	0	0	1	6	14–5	0.96
7/30	@New York	7–1	9.0	5	1	1	1	8	15–5	0.96
8/4	Chicago	5–6	11.0	12	5	4	3	10	ND	1.08
8/9	@Atlanta	1–0	9.0	4	0	0	0	5	16–5	1.04
8/14	@Chicago	3–1	9.0	8	1	1	3	7	17–5	1.04
8/19	@Philadelphia	2–0	9.0	2	0	0	2	11	18–5	1.00
8/24	Pittsburgh	4–6	9.0	6	6	3	2	15	18–6	1.07
8/28	@Pittsburgh	8–0	9.0	4	0	0	3	14	19–6	1.03
9/2	@Cincinnati	1–0	10.0	4	0	0	3	8	20–6	0.99
9/6	San Francisco	2–3	8.0	9	3	2	0	7	20–7	1.03
9/11	Los Angeles	5–4	9.0	11	4	4	2	6	21–7	1.13
9/17	@San Francisco	0–1	8.0	4	1	1	2	10	21–8	1.13
9/22	@Los Angeles	2–3	8.0	7	3	2	5	11	21–9	1.16
9/27	Houston	1–0	9.0	6	0	0	0	11	22–9	1.12

Cardinal Bill White singled in the game's only run with two outs and runners on first and second. As summer approached, Gibson was somehow 3–5 with an ERA of 1.52. He'd have to get even better, and since he was Bob Gibson, he would.

June 2 in New York the Cardinals gave him six runs to bump him to 4–5, but it was his complete-game shutout in Houston later that week that announced the beginning of the most incredible run any pitcher has ever had. Until he allowed four runs in a 13-inning loss in Chicago two months later, Gibson simply could not be beaten.

During those two months, by every measure, Gibson pitched as well as it is possible to pitch.

Opponents hit just .163 against him, and it wasn't hard contact. They slugged .190. In 99 innings—he completed every game in this 11-start stretch, of course— he struck out 83 and allowed just

Redbird Reference

Adam Wainwright

Adam Wainwright's most indelible moments as a Cardinal came as the team's surprise relief ace in the 2006 postseason, but few were surprised when that inning-at-a-time phenom turned into one of the top workhorses of the National League.

Before he became the set-up man and eventual closer of the World Champion 2006 Cardinals, Wainwright was a prospect whose can't-miss career had been waylaid by injuries ever since he'd arrived in AAA Memphis. It was only after a strong Spring Training vaulted him into the bullpen that all was forgiven, and it was only after Jason Isringhausen's ineffectiveness vaulted Wainwright into the closer's role in the NLCS against the heavily favored Mets that fans began to expect great things again for the lanky curveball specialist they'd been following for two years in the minor leagues.

But it was Game 7 of that series when Wainwright became a permanent part of Cardinals history. With two outs in the bottom of the ninth inning, the bases loaded, and the Cardinals clinging to a 3–1 lead, Carlos Beltran, the Cardinals' longtime postseason bogeyman, stepped to the plate with a chance to advance his Mets to the World Series for the first time since 2000.

Instead, Adam Wainwright threw the most perfect pitch of his career, an 0–2 curveball that dove out of the air and just caught the outside edge of the plate. Beltran, who'd hit seven heartbreaking home runs in 14 postseason games against the Cardinals, could only watch as it was called for strike three. A little more than a week later Wainwright would get Brandon Inge swinging to bring the Cardinals their first World Series championship since 1982.

As important as he was in 2006, Wainwright proved to be even better as a starter. In 2009 the former closer led the league in innings pitched, games started, and wins, and in 2010 he won 20 games for the first time while setting a career low with a 2.42 ERA. The end of the World Series, it turns out, was only the beginning of Adam Wainwright's career.

56 hits. Altogether he allowed just three runs; at one point, from June 6 to June 26, he threw five consecutive shutouts. From 4–5 he reached 15–5 before receiving a no decision in that August 4 loss—he threw 11 innings in the sauna that was Busch Stadium before leaving the game for a reliever.

Being lifted for a pinch-hitter was rare enough, but at least he did it on occasion—not a single time in 1968 was Bob Gibson pulled in the middle of an inning. On the days Gibson was pitching, everyone else on the Cardinals—the relievers and the position players—was just a little less necessary. Shortstop Dal Maxvill compared it to having the night off every fifth day, and he remembered a time when he walked over to Gibson to calm him down after a runner had reached base. "Get out of here," Gibson said. "The only thing you know about pitching is that it's hard to hit."

It's difficult to slice the numbers in a way that doesn't make Gibson look phenomenal. In his 22 victories—all complete games—he carried an ERA of 0.57. In his nine losses—he only completed six of those, the bum—his ERA ballooned to 2.14. During the day his ERA was 1.59; at night it was 0.93. Against teams with losing records, 1.03; with winning records, 1.25. The five times he pitched on three days' rest he threw four shutouts, carried an ERA of 0.41, and somehow lost one game.

As late as September 2, Gibson's ERA was less than 1, thanks to a 10-inning shutout in Cincinnati, and his regular season ended fittingly enough—he threw a shutout September 27 against Houston, to win by a score of 1–0 when no one but Curt Flood, who drove in the game's only run, could reach 12–15 Larry Dierker. Gibson finished the season with nine losses, 22 wins, and an impossible 1.12 ERA, nearly an entire run

Bob Gibson's World Series Game-By-Game Performance

Date	WS Game	Opponent	Result	IP	H	R	ER	BB	K
10/8/64	2	New York	L, 3–8	8.0	8	4	4	3	9
10/12/64	5	@New York	W, 5–2	10.0	6	2	0	2	13
10/15/64	7	New York	W, 7–5	9.0	9	5	5	3	9
10/4/67	1	@Boston	W, 2–1	9.0	6	1	1	1	10
10/8/67	4	Boston	W, 6–0	9.0	5	0	0	1	6
10/12/67	7	@Boston	W, 7–2	9.0	3	2	2	3	10
10/2/68	1	Detroit	W, 4–0	9.0	5	0	0	1	17
10/6/68	4	@Detroit	W, 10–1	9.0	5	1	1	2	10
10/10/68	7	Detroit	L, 1–4	9.0	8	4	4	1	8

ahead of his closest National League competitor.

His aura of invincibility carried into the World Series where the Cardinals—ahead of their nearest National League competitor by nine games—faced the 103-win Detroit Tigers, whose ace was also having a special season. Denny McLain, just 24 years old, had won 31 games, the first 30-game-winner since the Cardinals' Dizzy Dean more than 30 years earlier. Both pitchers would be named the MVP of their respective leagues; both had pitching lines more

Single-Game Pitching Records Since 1920

Record	Total	Pitcher, Date, Opponent
Most Strikeouts	19	Steve Carlton, 9/15/1969, vs. New York
Most Strikeouts, Relief	10	Dizzy Dean, 8/21/1932, vs. Boston
Most Walks	10	Syl Johnson, 7/12/1929, @Brooklyn
		Bill Hallahan, 7/31/1929, vs. Brooklyn
		Bill Hallahan, 5/1/1932, @Chicago
		Steve Carlton, 7/3/1971, @San Francisco
		Jeff Suppan, 7/28/2004, @Cincinnati
Most Runs Allowed	16	Johnny Stuart, 6/22/1925, vs. Pittsburgh
Most Hits Allowed	21	Bill Sherdel, 7/3/1929, @Pittsburgh
Most Home Runs Allowed	5	Scott Terry, 6/4/1989, vs. Chicago
		Harvey Haddix, 6/27/1954, @Brooklyn
Most Innings Pitched	17.0	Dizzy Dean, 7/1/1934, @Cincinnati
		Roy Parmelee, 4/29/1936, vs. New York Giants
Highest Game Score	116	Roy Parmelee, 4/29/1936, vs. New York Giants
Highest Game Score, 9 IP	97	Ernie Broglio, 7/15/1960, vs. Chicago

Strikeouts in a Single Season, Since 1901

Rank	Pitcher	SO	Year
1.	Bob Gibson	274	1970
2.	Bob Gibson	270	1965
3.	Bob Gibson	269	1969
4.	Bob Gibson	268	1968
5.	Bob Gibson	245	1964
6.	Sam Jones	225	1958
	Bob Gibson	225	1966
8.	Chris Carpenter	213	2005
	Adam Wainwright	213	2010
10.	Adam Wainwright	212	2009

Best Single-Season Earned Run Average

Rank	Pitcher	ERA	Year
1.	Bob Gibson	1.12	1968
2.	Silver King	1.63	1888
3.	Bill Doak	1.72	1914
4.	Mort Cooper	1.78	1942
5.	Max Lanier	1.90	1943
6.	John Tudor	1.93	1985
7.	Kid Nichols	2.02	1904
8.	Bugs Raymond	2.03	1908
9.	Ed Karger	2.04	1907
10.	Bob Caruthers	2.07	1885

reminiscent of the dead ball era than anything fans had seen in 50 years.

And McLain just never had a chance. The Cardinals put three runs on him in the fourth inning when Roger Maris' leadoff walk teed off a rally carried out by Mike Shannon and Julian Javier, and the 31-game-winner was removed after the fifth inning, by which time Gibson had already struck out nine batters, including star Al Kaline twice.

While McLain sat in the dugout, Gibson seemed to only get better. In the sixth inning, with runners on second and third and slugger Norm Cash at the plate, Gibson picked up his 11th strikeout to end their last scoring threat. In the seventh, he struck out two more batters, and in the eighth he fanned pinch-hitter Eddie Mathews to reach 14, one short of Sandy Koufax's World Series record.

Gibby came out in the ninth with the middle of the order in front of him one last time and more trouble than he'd seen in a while. When second-place hitter Mickey Stanley hit a line drive single to lead off the inning, he was the first Tiger to reach base since the sixth, and he had Kaline, Cash, and Willie Horton batting behind him. Kaline had been on a tear since late August, hitting .379 down the stretch after returning from an injury. He

Behind the Numbers

Mort Cooper, the 1942 National League MVP, was the pitching ace behind the great Cardinals teams of the World War II period, winning 20 games three consecutive seasons between 1942 and 1944. His 23 shutouts over that span were 10 more than the next best pitcher.

became Gibson's Koufax-tying 15th victim. Cash had hit 25 home runs, seemingly unaffected by the pitching-friendly environment of 1968; he went down next, and although Gibson had to be told by catcher Tim McCarver that he'd broken the record it didn't take long for the Busch faithful to erupt. After play resumed, Willie Horton—who'd hit a career-high 36 home runs in that inhospitable season—stood up to face Gibson and promptly, famously struck out looking.

The final tally: Nine innings pitched; five hits, one walk, and no runs allowed; 17 of 32 batters down on strikes. Gibson hadn't only outdueled Denny McLain that afternoon in Busch Stadium; he'd outdueled everyone who'd ever had the chance to pitch in the World Series. He beat the struggling McLain again in Game 5, but after six scoreless innings in Game 7 Gibby finally blinked, allowing a two-out triple that scored two runs and ended his postseason career on a sour note when the Cardinals couldn't come back against Series MVP Mickey Lolich.

Even with that final loss Gibson remains one of the most brilliant World Series performers of all time. In nine World Series starts he threw eight complete games and two shutouts, struck out 92 batters against just 55 hits, and went 7–2 with an ERA of 1.89. It's the equivalent of a perfect relief season tacked on to his 251–174 career record, and it came in baseball's highest-pressure situations.

Gibson was one of baseball's best pitchers for another five years, winning his second Cy Young Award with a career-high 23 wins

Behind the Numbers

To win the Pitcher's Triple Crown, a starter must lead the league in wins, ERA, and strikeouts in the same season. No Cardinal has ever accomplished the feat, although several have won two legs of the Triple Crown—from Bob Caruthers in 1885 to Bob Gibson in 1968.

in 1970, but he had already made his point. When a game was on the line and the offense wasn't carrying its weight, there was no pitcher more eager for the assignment than Gibson—and no pitcher more capable of carrying it out.

Shutouts in a Single Season

Rank	Player	SHO	Year
1.	Bob Gibson	13	1968
2.	Dave Foutz	11	1886
3.	Mort Cooper	10	1942
	John Tudor	10	1985
5.	Bill Doak	7	1914
	Dizzy Dean	7	1934
	Mort Cooper	7	1944
	Harry Brecheen	7	1948
9.	10 pitchers, most recently		
	Bob Gibson	6	1965

Cardinals Strikeout Champions

Year	Player	Strikeouts
1891†	Jack Stivets	259
1906	Fred Beebe	116
1930	Bill Hallahan	177
1931	Bill Hallahan	159
1932	Dizzy Dean	191
1933	Dizzy Dean	199
1934	Dizzy Dean	195
1935	Dizzy Dean	190
1948	Harry Brecheen	149
1958	Sam Jones	225
1968	Bob Gibson	268
1989	Jose DeLeon	201

Cardinals Wins Champions

Year	Player	Wins
1885†	Bob Caruthers	40
1886†	Dave Foutz	41
1888†	Silver King	45
1926	Flint Rhem	20
1931	Bill Hallahan	19
1934	Dizzy Dean	30
1935	Dizzy Dean	28
1942	Mort Cooper	22
1943	Mort Cooper	21
1945	Red Barrett	21
1946	Howie Pollett	21
1960	Ernie Broglio	21
1970	Bob Gibson	23
1984	Joaquin Andujar	20
2001	Matt Morris	22
2009	Adam Wainwright	19

Cardinals ERA Champions

Year	Player	ERA
1885†	Bob Caruthers	2.07
1886†	Dave Foutz	2.11
1888†	Silver King	1.63
1889†	Jack Stivetts	2.25
1893	Ted Breitenstein	3.18
1914	Bill Doak	1.72
1921	Bill Doak	2.59
1942	Mort Cooper	1.78
1943	Max Lanier	1.90
1946	Howie Pollet	2.10
1948	Harry Brecheen	2.24
1968	Bob Gibson	1.12
1976	John Denny	2.52
1988	Joe Magrane	2.18
2009	Chris Carpenter	2.24

†: Player led the American Association in ERA.

CHAPTER 7

DIZZY DEAN WINS 30 GAMES FOR THE GASHOUSE GANG

More Cardinals Pitching Records

One of the perils of being Dizzy Dean—not that he must have minded—was being more famous for how you talked about what you did than what you did. Dean, first as a player and later as one of the most popular broadcasters in baseball, could tell you what he did in a much more interesting way than any encyclopedia; he had a quote for every possible situation.

On getting shelled: "[Bill Terry] once hit a ball between my legs so hard that my center-fielder caught it on the fly backing up against the wall."

On losing his effectiveness: "I ain't what I used to be, but who the hell is?"

On being great: Too many to list. "It ain't braggin' if you can back it up," and "Anybody who's ever had the privilege of seeing me play knows

that I am the greatest pitcher in the world," are a good start.

He had plenty to say about his relatively taciturn brother, too. After Paul "Daffy" Dean follow Dizzy's three-hit shutout with a no-hitter in the second game of a doubleheader, Diz was the center of attention, delivering this vote of self-confidence right to waiting reporters: "Gee, Paul, if I'd-a known you was gonna throw a no-hitter, I'd-a thrown one, too!"

He even had the final word on his famous malapropisms, saying, "The good Lord was good to me. He gave me a strong body, a good right arm, and a weak mind." There might never have been a newspaper headline reading "X-Ray of Dean's Head Reveals Nothing," but once the rumor got around you can be sure Dean acted as though it was the gospel truth.

Dizzy Dean was a great talker, but he's so famous for it mostly because he was an even better pitcher. In 1934 he proved himself to be the greatest talker and pitcher in baseball—and if you didn't believe it, you only had to ask him.

By 1934 Dean, only 24 years old, had already established himself as one of the best sources in baseball for fastballs and column inches. In 1932, his rookie season, he led baseball in innings pitched and strikeouts and false

Behind The Numbers

In the 1800s pitchers often pitched half of their team's games in a given season—the distance from what was then called the "pitcher's box" to home plate was shorter than it is now, but careers were still often nasty, brutish, and short—and especially prone to dominating teams' all-time pitching leaderboards.

information fed to reporters. When pressed on the matter of his multiple birthdays and twin sets of given names (Jay Hanna and Jerome Herman), Dean said, "Them's not lies. Them's scoops."

Reporters were willing to print the legend and not the fact so long as Diz kept his end of the bargain and backed it up—and in 1933 he was even better. This time the Cardinals were better, too. Frankie Frisch became player-manager midway through the season, and the Cardinals finished with 82 wins after a disappointing 1932.

That July Dean made his first mark on the national stage when he took the mound at Sportsman's Park for the first game of a doubleheader with the Cubs. With Frisch newly installed at the helm and the Cardinals on a five-game winning streak, Dean punctuated their newfound resolve by striking out 17 Cubs in nine innings, a new MLB record. "Heck," he said, unwilling to do anything without immortalizing it in his own prose, "if anybody told me I was setting a record, I'd of got me some more strikeouts." Dean would finish the season with 199 strikeouts, which again led the league, and 20 wins.

But it wasn't until 1934 that the Cardinals would internalize Dean's dizziness and become the team that would be known forever-more as the Gashouse Gang—a group of rough, undereducatedeven-for-1930s baseball players baseball players who played with a strange combination of aggressive intensity and flippant jokiness that was infuriating, unless you were a Cardinals fan. Dizzy Dean was their conscience, their ringleader, and their public spokesman, and while he'd already become one of the most visible pitchers in baseball, it was still a surprise when he became one of the very best.

Well, it was a surprise to anyone who hadn't talked to Dizzy Dean. Before the season, his younger brother Paul—reluctantly nicknamed "Daffy"—had joined the Cardinals, and Diz had graciously told reporters that "Me 'n Paul," as he named them, would combine to win 45 games.

Given Paul's age and inexperience, that would require at least 25 wins from Diz, and for a while it looked like neither Dean was up to the task—they combined for one win in April that year, with Paul pitching just six innings in long relief and Diz going 1–2 with a 7.17 ERA.

In April Diz looked foolish, but in May he looked eerily farsighted—it ain't clairvoyance, it turns out, if you can back it up. On May 3 Paul, taking his second start of the year, got blown out, allowing five runs in as many innings, but he picked up a win when Joe Medwick drove in five runs of his own. On May 5 Diz, who had thrown a relief inning

Behind the Numbers

Through the history of baseball, individual starting pitchers have consistently pitched fewer and fewer innings in a season, on average. The most innings any Cardinals starter has pitched since 2000, the 241.2 Chris Carpenter managed in 2005, ranks just 90th on the team's single-season list, while you have to get to 27th in team history to reach Kip Wells' 17 losses in 2007.

between starts to work out some kinks, allowed one run in five innings to pick up his second win of the season.

"Me 'n Paul" in 1934

Month	Dizzy Dean	Paul Dean
April	1	0
May	5	5
June	6	5
July	6	1
August	5	3
September	7	5
TOTAL	**30**	**19**

That month neither of the Cardinals' two Deans could be beaten. Paul won five consecutive starts despite dealing with some growing pains, while Diz was as ubiquitous as he was difficult to hit—he won all five of his starts and finished three more games, picking up two saves decades before anyone would realize what

Redbird Reference

Chris Carpenter

After the 2003 season, Cardinals fans disappointed by a narrow third-place finish in the National League Central needed only to look at the rotation, a patchwork group comprised mostly of failed bets on veteran arms, when it came time to point the blame. Brett Tomko, an erstwhile top prospect who'd had limited success in the major leagues, led the NL in hits and earned runs allowed. Garrett Stephenson, a hero in the 2000 regular season, never quite recovered from elbow surgery.

But the most frustrating of all the Cardinals' bad bets had to be Chris Carpenter, an ex-Blue-Jays starter who had *already had shoulder surgery* when the Cardinals signed him to a two-year contract. The idea was that he'd rehab and give the rotation a boost in midseason; instead, he just vanished, missing the entire year and serving in absentia as a symbol for a squandered season.

Nobody expected much out of Carpenter in 2004, and from that moment on he managed to meet all those limited expectations people did have—he suffered a major shoulder injury, ate a ton of innings on the occasions that he was healthy, and served as an extremely vocal presence on the field and in the dugout. Of course, he also made himself into one of the best pitchers in Major League Baseball—twice.

From the moment he arrived at Busch Stadium, he was a different pitcher. A perpetual prospect in Toronto—the kind of pitcher people always expect a little more out of—Carpenter seemed to relish having no expectations at all in St. Louis.

Cardinals fans quickly saw what had made Toronto fans so alternately hopeful and disappointed, and whether it was the surgery or Dave Duncan's pitching philosophy, something had changed in Carpenter during his rehab. His mid-nineties fastball always seemed to tail back over the outside corner of the strikezone, no matter where he threw it, and the moment a batter looked for it, Carpenter reared back for a hard curveball or the Dave Duncan special, a baffling cutter the Cardinals pitching coach seemed to teach his every pupil.

But nobody took to Duncan's plan quite as well as Chris Carpenter, who combined his pitching coach's pitch-to-contact mantra with pitches that made it extremely difficult for hitters to make contact. His problems with control and hitability vanished, and in 2004 "Carp" struck out four batters for every one he walked, one of the best ratios in baseball, on his way to a 15–5 record. A nerve problem knocked out the Cardinals' unlikely ace just before the end of the regular season, and some fans still blame the hole at the top of their rotation for the Boston Red Sox's four-game sweep that October.

Shoulder and nerve problems in consecutive years had the Cardinals worried enough about their new star that they traded for Mark Mulder in the 2005 offseason, looking for a more conventional number-one starter. But Carpenter looked anything but fragile that year, pitching four shutouts and leading the major leagues with seven complete games. Carpenter's 21–5 record and his 241 innings pitched—second in baseball—earned him the honor of the National League Cy Young Award that year in a narrow victory over Marlins sensation Dontrelle Willis.

But it wasn't until 2006 that Carpenter would finally be able to make up for that lost World Series start. After propelling the 83-win Cardinals into the NLCS with two brilliant starts against the San Diego Padres, Carpenter took the mound in Game 3 of the World Series against the heavily favored Detroit Tigers with the series tied at one.

Nobody was better suited to pitch the first game of the series at Busch Stadium, and Carpenter didn't disappoint, stifling the Tigers' offense over eight scoreless innings and turning the momentum permanently in the Cardinals' favor on their way to a 3–1 series victory and their first championship since 1982.

Already Carpenter's career was stuffed full of more highlights than most. After elbow problems struck in 2007, he could have retired and still become a Cardinals legend. Instead, he fought his way back. Over two grueling years of rehab, and two aborted attempts at a comeback, Carpenter returned to the Cardinals in 2009 somehow exactly as good as he'd been before, going 17–4 with a league-leading 2.24 ERA and nearly winning a second Cy Young.

A 16-win season in 2010 cemented Chris Carpenter's unusual legacy forever. Most pitchers don't return from shoulder problems once, and fewer still come back better than they were before. Carpenter—as grim as his prospects looked after that lost 2003 season—did it twice.

those were. Suddenly the Deans had gone from one win to 11 and from a laughingstock to two pitchers with a very real chance of winning 22.5 a piece.

They were certainly doing their part, but Diz must also have counted on the Cardinals' offense, which proved itself to be the best in the National League. First baseman Ripper Collins and second-year outfielder Joe Medwick each drove in more than 100 runs and the Cardinals finished with a league-leading 799 of them. ("Me 'n Paul," it should be said, did their part—they combined to hit .244 with two home runs and 21 runs scored.)

As a result, even when a Dean got beaten he didn't necessarily, well, get beaten. On June 26 Paul picked up his 10th win of the season despite allowing seven runs and 15 hits in his nine innings; the next day Diz earned his 12th by allowing seven runs and 12 hits in 8⅔ innings.

On July 1, when Diz went 17 innings, allowed six runs, and won for the 13th time that season, the brothers had gotten more than halfway to their goal—and they'd done it just 66 games into the season.

That meant the family goal of 45 wins was well within reach, but it also meant that Dizzy Dean could do something nobody in the National League had managed since 1917—he was on pace to win 30 games almost exactly. The last NL star to do it had been Pete Alexander in 1917, and just two American Leaguers had done it in the years since.

He would have to keep going at his Herculean pace to reach the mark, but as summer bore down on St. Louis, Diz was getting better with every start. One dominant stretch in the middle of July saw him strike out 10 in a complete-game win against Cincinnati, relieve Paul to win a game at Philadelphia with eight strikeouts

Single-Season Winning Percentage

Rank	Player	W–L%	Record	Year
1.	Dizzy Dean	.811	30–7	1934
2.	Ted Wilks	.810	17–4	1944
	Chris Carpenter	.810	17–4	2009
4.	Chris Carpenter	.808	21–5	2005
5.	Harry Brecheen	.789	15–4	1945
6.	Johnny Beazley	.778	21–6	1942
7.	Bob Gibson	.767	23–7	1970
8.	Jesse Haines	.765	13–4	1926
9.	Bob Caruthers	.763	29–9	1887
10.	Bob Tewksbury	.762	16–5	1992

in 3⅔ scoreless innings a few days later, and then—in his regular start—throw a four-hit shutout to sneak past Brooklyn and improve to 16–3 by July 15.

Paul was struggling, at least by comparison; after getting blown out early in the month, the Cardinals held him out of a few starts and he won just one game, moving to 11–4. By August he had returned to the rotation, but it seemed for a while like Diz would win 45 without him—that month he won five games with an ERA of just 1.41, throwing two more of his league-leading seven shutouts.

On September 1 "Me 'n Paul" had 37 wins—23 from Me, 14 from Paul and the Cardinals, more importantly, were 5.5 games behind the New York Giants,

defending World Series champions, for the NL pennant. The Giants had taken the lead in June and held onto it for most of the season, and on September 4 they ran seven games ahead of the Cardinals, their biggest margin of the season.

It was a lucky thing for the Cardinals that their own pennant chase coincided with the Deans' personal goals. On September 9 Paul threw a shutout in the first game of a victorious doubleheader to bring the Cardinals within five; the next day Diz won his 25th game to bring the margin to four.

On September 21 the Deans cut the Giants' lead to 3.5 games with one of the most impressive pitching feats Me-'n-anybody-else have ever achieved. In the first of two games at Brooklyn's Ebbets

Single-Season Pitching Records

Category	Number	Player, Year
Most Wins	45	Silver King, 1888
Most Wins Since 1901	30	Dizzy Dean, 1934
Most Saves	47	Jason Isringhausen, 2004
Most Games	89	Steve Kline, 2001
Games Started	64	Silver King, 1888
Games Started Since 1901	41	Bob Harmon, 1911
Complete Games Since 1901	39	Jack Taylor, 1904
Innings Pitched Since 1901	352.1	Stoney McGlynn, 1907
Lowest ERA	1.12	Bob Gibson, 1968
Most Strikeouts Since 1901	274	Bob Gibson, 1970
Most Shutouts	13	Bob Gibson, 1968
Winning Percentage	.811	Dizzy Dean, 1934
Most Losses Since 1901	25	Bugs Raymond, 1908
Home Runs Allowed	39	Murry Dickson, 1948
Most Walks Since 1901	181	Bob Harmond, 1911
Most Hit Batsmen Since 1901	18	Willie Sudhoff, 1901
Most Wild Pitches Since 1901	19	Jack Harper, 1901

Field, the Cardinals got out in front early, putting up seven runs for Diz is the first three innings behind six RBIs from Ripper Collins. The Cardinals' offense would finish with 13 runs, but Diz only needed the one—he threw a three-hit shutout, striking out seven Dodgers.

It was the second-best game a Cardinals pitcher born in Lucas, Arkansas, would pitch that afternoon. Paul went 2–3 with a double and scored a run on Pepper Martin's single, which proved to be two more hits and one more run than the Dodgers would manage for the rest of the day. Backed up by a relatively sedate three runs, Paul threw the Cardinals' first no-hitter in 10 years.

Diz, of course, acted as sibling spokesman once more.

As good as they'd been all year, he just might have. The three-hitter was Diz's 27th win and the no-hitter Paul's 18th win—leaving them with 45 wins exactly. Diz's prediction had come true, but the Cardinals were still in second place. They needed to make up 3½ wins on the Giants, and as it turned out the Deans had exactly four wins left in their right arms.

On the 25th Diz won his 28th game to bring the Cardinals within one, and in their last homestand against Cincinnati, manager Frankie Frisch brought out Deans in their final three games with the National League pennant in

the balance. On September 28 Diz shut out the Reds behind two RBIs each from Medwick and Leo Durocher to tie the NL pennant race for the first time since June 5.

On September 29, with the Giants down 5–1 against the bottom-dwelling Brooklyn Dodgers at the Polo Grounds, Paul gave the Cardinals the lead with a complete-game win of his own, his 19th victory.

And on September 30, pitching on one day's rest for the third time in as many starts, Diz threw a shutout, winning his 30th game of the season and clinching the pennant for the Gashouse Gang on the last day of the season.

"Me 'n Paul" and the rest of the Gashouse Gang had less than a week to celebrate before traveling to Detroit where the 101-win Tigers had wrapped up the pennant a month earlier.

The Tigers had the wins and an even more dangerous offense, but they were out-Deaned two to none. Game 1 saw Diz go the distance for the win, while in Game 3 Paul threw eight shutout innings to put the Cardinals up 2–1. In Game 5 Tommy Bridges outdueled Diz, but there was just too many of them. Paul won Game 6 against Schoolboy Rowe and Diz threw a shutout in Game 7, and the World Series was over, Deans 4, Tigers 3.

Paul won 19 games just one more time before succumbing to

Cardinals 20-Game Winners

Year	Pitcher	Record	Year	Pitcher	Record
1882†	Jumbo McGinnis	25–18	1933	Dizzy Dean	20–18
1883†	Tony Mullane	35–15	1934	Dizzy Dean	30–7
	Jumbo McGinnis	28–16	1935	Dizzy Dean	28–12
1884†	Jumbo McGinnis	24–16	1936	Dizzy Dean	24–13
1885†	Dave Foutz	33–14	1939	Curt Davis	22–16
	Bob Caruthers	40–13	1942	Johnny Beazley	21–6
1886†	Dave Foutz	41–16		Mort Cooper	22–7
	Bob Caruthers	30–14	1943	Mort Cooper	21–8
1887†	Dave Foutz	25–12	1944	Mort Cooper	22–7
	Bob Caruthers	29–9	1945	Red Barrett	21–9
	Silver King	32–12	1946	Howie Pollet	21–10
1888†	Silver King	45–20	1948	Harry Brecheen	20–7
	Nat Hudson	25–10	1949	Howie Pollet	20–9
1889†	Silver King	35–16	1953	Harvey Haddix	20–9
	Ice Box Chamberlain	32–15	1960	Ernie Broglio	21–9
1890†	Toad Ramsey	23–17	1964	Ray Sadecki	20–11
	Jack Stivetts	27–21	1965	Bob Gibson	20–12
1891†	Jack Stivetts	33–22	1966	Bob Gibson	21–12
1892	Kid Gleason	20–24	1968	Bob Gibson	22–9
1893	Kid Gleason	21–22	1969	Bob Gibson	20–13
1894	Ted Breitenstein	27–23	1970	Bob Gibson	23–7
1899	Cy Young	26–16	1971	Steve Carlton	20–9
1901	Jack Harper	23–13	1977	Bob Forsch	20–7
1904	Kid Nichols	21–13	1984	Joaquin Andujar	20–14
	Jack Taylor	20–19	1985	Joaquin Andujar	21–12
1911	Bob Harmon	23–16		John Tudor	21–8
1920	Bill Doak	20–12	2000	Darryl Kile	20–9
1923	Jesse Haines	20–13	2001	Matt Morris	22–8
1926	Flint Rhem	20–7	2005	Chris Carpenter	21–5
1927	Pete Alexander	21–10	2010	Adam Wainwright	20–11
	Jesse Haines	24–10			
1928	Jesse Haines	20–8			
	Bill Sherdel	21–10			

injuries, and Diz seemed to stick around exactly long enough to establish his legacy as the casually outstanding superstar of the Gashouse Gang. After a 28 win season in 1935 and 24 wins in 1936, disaster struck at the 1937 All-Star Game, his fourth in a row.

Diz, starting for the National League, was struck on the foot by an Earl Averill comebacker, fracturing his big toe. He got the out to end the third inning, but according to baseball lore it was the end for Dizzy Dean's run as the terror of the National League.

Coming back too early—he was on the mound on July 21, two weeks after the incident, when he allowed two runs in eight innings—led him to change his mechanics to favor the toe, and the new motion ruined his rubber arm.

Diz was effective the rest of the season—he went 2–2 with an ERA of 3.59—but his strikeout rate fell from 6.61 batters per nine innings before the injury, which would have been a new career high, to just 1.89, one of the lowest in all of baseball. Picked up by the Chicago Cubs after the season, Dean played perhaps the best practical joke of his storied Cardinals career—his fastball, and the strikeouts, never came back, and the Cubs got just 226 innings and 16 wins out of their $185,000 investment.

Dizzy Dean, meanwhile, had been exactly brilliant enough to become America's favorite baseball broadcaster. By 1950 he was broadcasting the national game of the week on TV, delivering his malapropisms directly to his public without need of any reporters. To a later generation of baseball fans, Dean was as famous for the strange contortions of his vocabulary—a player "slud" into third base in the past tense, and there was no greater defender of the word *ain't*—as for his brilliant pitching.

Of course, he wouldn't want people to think he gave it up voluntarily. In 1947, covering radio duties for the beleaguered St. Louis Browns, Diz's mouth managed, for neither the first time nor the last, to get him into trouble. After criticizing the Browns' pitching staff all year from the booth, the permanently poor Browns sensed a publicity coup and brought him in to pitch on the last day of the season.

At 37 years old and visibly in broadcaster's shape—he hadn't pitched in more than six years—a more rotund Diz huffed and puffed to the mound to pitch against the Chicago White Sox

Most Innings Pitched Since 1901

Rank	Player	Innings Pitched	Year
1.	Stoney McGlynn	352.1	1907
2.	Jack Taylor	352.0	1904
3.	Bob Harmon	348.0	1911
4.	Jack Powell	338.1	1901
5.	Dizzy Dean	325.1	1935
6.	Bugs Raymond	324.1	1908
7.	Kid Nichols	317.0	1904
8.	Dizzy Dean	315.0	1936
9.	Ed Karger	314.0	1907
	Bob Gibson		1969

Most Losses in a Single Season

Rank	Player	Losses	Year
1.	Red Donahue	35	1897
2.	Ted Breitenstein	30	1895
3.	Bill Hart	29	1896
	Jack Taylor		1898
5.	Pink Hawley	27	1894
	Bill Hart		1897
	Willie Sudhoff		1898
8.	Ted Breitenstein	26	1896
9.	Stoney McGlynn	25	1907
	Bugs Raymond		1908

in front of about 16,000 fans at Sportsman's Park. His fastball was anything but, and his build precluded him picking up his 24th double or fifth triple, but as it turned out there was just a little more Dizzy Dean left in the tube. Diz pitched four scoreless innings and pulled a muscle singling in his only at-bat, which he took as a sign to return to the booth for good.

Dizzy Dean the ballplayer had made his last appearance, but it wasn't official until he handed things back over to Dizzy Dean the talker. Talking to reporters after the game, he explained, "I said I could pitch as good as most of these fellers, and I can. But I'll be doggoned if I'm gonna ever try again. Talking's my game now, and I'm just glad that muscle I pulled wasn't in my throat."

CHAPTER 8

BOB FORSCH THROWS TWO
NO-HITTERS FOR THE CARDINALS
Cardinals No-Hitters

Few pitchers—let alone former 20-game winners—seemed less likely to throw a no-hitter than Bob Forsch, a control-minded innings-eater who shored up the Cardinals' rotation for 15 seasons as the rare sure thing in one of the most ephemeral roles in baseball. In a 16-year career Forsch struck out 100 batters all of three times while allowing more than 200 hits eight times. His career strikeout rate of 3.6 per nine innings isn't just low—it's the lowest of any pitcher since 1970 who earned at least 150 wins.

But there he was, on September 26, 1983, with a mostly empty Busch Stadium roaring and Manny Trillo at the plate, just one out away from his second no-hitter in five years—and the third Forsch family no-hitter.

Maybe we should back up. In 1977 Forsch, 27, had emerged as a 20-game winner on a third-place Cardinals squad that seemed to offer endless promise for 1978. Ted Simmons, 27 himself, had hit .318 with 21 home runs; Keith Hernandez, 23, hit .291 and drove in 91 runs; Garry Templeton, 21, rapped 200 hits and 18 triples in the first full season of his career.

That year Forsch had anchored an even younger rotation and ridden the team's strong offense to the Cardinals' first 20-win season since Bob Gibson and Steve Carlton had departed.

In 1978 things didn't work out quite as planned for Forsch or the Cardinals, but on April 16 the Cardinals held themselves together long enough for him to pitch the

Redbird Reference

Jesse Haines

Jesse "Pop" Haines is a Hall of Famer—for some reason—but this might be the most improbable no-hitter in Cardinals history, Jose Jimenez included. In the four games after his July 17 no-hitter against the Boston Braves, Pop allowed 15, 12, 12, and 10 hits. All told he gave up 10 hits or more 12 times that year, in 31 starts, and despite the advantage of having allowed zero in one other start he finished fourth in the National League that year with 275.

Altogether it was not a great time to be Pop Haines. Like Forsch he was coming off a 20-win season he was not about to repeat, and he came into the no-hitter with a 5–12 record and an ERA to match. But that day Haines was nearly perfect, striking out five batters—somehow a season high—and walking three.

That's the kind of pitcher Haines was, at his best and his worst. A Cardinal for 18 years, Haines won 20 games three times and spent six seasons at the back of the Gashouse Gang's bullpen, and the whole time he was a contact pitcher with no fastball and a strange variation on the knuckleball.

He won 210 games, pitched until he was 43, and won two games in the Cardinals' first ever World Series championship in 1926. But he's most famous for his no-hitter, the least characteristic thing Pop ever did. He's most famous for *somehow*, despite allowing 3,460 in his career, going for one of his 386 career starts without allowing a single hit.

Contemporary Comparo: I know this to be true—if Jeff Suppan had pitched for 18 years without getting any better or worse than usual the entire time, he would have been nicknamed "Pop."

Bob Forschiest no-hitter of all time—no small feat considering he would eventually be competing against another Bob Forsch no-hitter.

Forsch had already won two of the Cardinals' four games that year, including a complete game on April 12 where he showed the closest thing to no-hit stuff he'd ever manage—against the Pittsburgh Pirates he'd struck out nine batters and walked three but allowed four hits.

From the moment his fated start began he set a much more familiar tone, retiring the Phillies in order on a groundout and two fly balls, including a loud Mike Schmidt out to Tony Scott in center field. After the Cardinals threatened but failed to score in the second, it was more of the same: two fly outs, one dribbler out past Ted Simmons, inning over.

In fact, neither team had a hit until the bottom of the fourth inning when Ted Simmons doubled off Phillies starter Randy Lerch and scored on a Ken Reitz single into the opposite field.

That prompted the most drama Forsch would face all game—Richie Hebner drew a one-out walk after yet another groundout and stole one of just four bases he'd nab all year, leaving Garry Maddox at the plate with the tying run in scoring position and just one out. Seemingly roused into action by the threat, Forsch struck out Maddox

Behind the Numbers

Bob Forsch was the only pitcher to throw a no-hitter at Busch Memorial Stadium—and he did it twice. He was the first Cardinals pitcher to throw a no-hitter at home since Jesse Haines 54 years earlier—and the last one to do it, nearly 30 years since.

and Bob Boone as though he were holding those swings-and-misses in reserve for a particularly important moment and promptly went back to being Bob Forsch again.

Three more runs in the sixth inning left Forsch with more slack than he'd need, and in the top of the seventh, almost abruptly, the Cardinals' ace was nine outs away from a no-hitter. Unfortunately, those nine outs meant he'd have to deal with Mike Schmidt, who'd already nearly taken him deep, one more time.

A more dramatic pitcher—a pitcher more befitting our no-hitter expectations—would have come face-to-face with Schmidt in the ninth inning with the game as well as the no-hitter on the line. But this was Bob Forsch, and drama wouldn't do—he saw him with one out in the seventh inning, Larry Bowa having just bounced one harmlessly back to the pitcher's mound.

For the second time the three-time home run champion

nearly broke the no-hitter and the shutout, flying deep to center field. But Jerry Mumphrey, who'd come into the game after the three-run rally, tracked it down, and Richie Hebner popped up to Garry Templeton at shortstop to end another quiet inning. The next inning saw more of the same anticlimax—Maddox reached with nobody out on Reitz's error, but Forsch got Bob Boone to ground into a 6-4-3 double play and that was that.

In the eighth inning, up 4–0 already, Forsch dealt with one of the most frustrating parts of any no-hitter—the late-innings, basically irrelevant home-team rally. With the top of the order up and the Phillies leaving Lerch in to absorb another round of punishment, the Cardinals got back-to-back hits from light-hitting outfielder Jerry Morales and Simmons. Sloppy infield play left them on second and third with nobody out, and Philadelphia finally went to its bullpen, causing another delay.

From there, as though determined to ice the proverbial kicker, the Phillies intentionally walked Keith Hernandez to load the bases and got outs from Reitz and Mumphrey. But Dane Iorg was brought in to pinch hit, and the slop continued—he walked to score the Cardinals' fifth run, rendering the Phillies' gamesmanship moot.

Behind the Numbers

Who else could plausibly claim to have pitched the best no-hitter in Cardinals history? For Gibson's no-hitter, in the midst of a season that saw him finish just 16–13, the future Hall of Famer finally got some run support, and he didn't even need it—that day he struck out 10 batters, including one who reached first base on a wild pitch, and walked three.

It came down, finally, to Forsch himself to end the inning—coming up with the bases loaded he hit a fly ball to center field to make the Cardinals' final out and then walked calmly out to the pitcher's mound to face the Phillies' order as it flipped over. If anyone reached base he'd have to face Mike Schmidt for a fourth time, but that just wouldn't have been right—instead he got three quick groundouts, and that was that.

Three strikeouts, two walks, four early runs, and just about two hours in front of a Busch Stadium crowd of little more than 11,000 fans. Not even a little fuss. That's how Bob Forsch pitches a no-hitter.

If he'd done it once, Forsch's brief transcendence of his steady reputation would have been an interesting footnote. But five years later, caught again in a down season for player and club, Forsch would return to the record book to sign his name once more.

It was September 26, 1983, and the defending World Series champions were 75–81, mired in the middle of the National League West. That year the Cardinals had put together one of their best offenses of the Whiteyball era—Lonnie Smith, Tommy Herr, and George Hendrick were on their

No Hitters Thrown by Cardinals Pitchers

Pitcher	Opponent	Date	Score	Game Score
Ted Breitenstein	Louisville Colonels	October 4, 1891	8–0	n/a
Jesse Haines	Boston Braves	July 17, 1924	5–0	89
Paul Dean	@ Brooklyn Dodgers	September 21, 1934	3–0	92
Lon Warneke	@ Cincinnati Reds	August 30, 1941	2–0	88
Ray Washburn	@ San Francisco Giants	September 18, 1968	2–0	90
Bob Gibson	@ Pittsburgh Pirates	August 14, 1971	11–0	94
Bob Forsch	Philadelphia Phillies	April 16, 1978	5–0	88
Bob Forsch	Montreal Expos	September 26, 1983	3–0	93
Jose Jimenez	@ Arizona Diamondbacks	June 25, 1999	1–0	93
Bud Smith	@ San Diego Padres	September 3, 2001	1–0	90

Recent No-Hitters in Cardinals History

In three years the Cardinals got two no-hitters from rookies who'd deliver them a combined 15 wins in their brief careers. The story began in 1999 when Jose Jimenez—who lost 14 games that year, with an ERA of 5.85—outdueled Randy Johnson by throwing a no-hitter in the Cardinals' 1–0 victory. The no-hitter was impressive enough, but the story got more improbable still 10 days later when Jimenez beat the eventual Cy Young winner 1–0 *again*, blanking the Diamondbacks with a two-hitter. That year saw Jimenez post a 0.00 ERA against Randy Johnson and a 6.58 ERA against everyone else.

Jimenez, who would eventually settle in as the Rockies' enigmatic closer, was a total surprise, but when Bud Smith emerged fully formed as a corner-hitting control artist, his no-hitter on September 3 in San Diego as well as the rest of his career seemed like a foregone conclusion.

Of course, things didn't quite turn out that way—Smith was out of baseball before Jimenez, a victim of shoulder problems that will always color his 134-pitch performance that night. But for one evening, he was everything the Cardinals could have hoped for.

way to career seasons—but the starting rotation had faltered all at once, and Forsch was no exception.

A year after he'd won 15 games—and then one more in the postseason, a three-hit shutout to open the NLCS—Forsch had spent much of the second half of 1983 with an ERA approaching 5.00. At the time he was coming off one of his worst stretches of the year, with three consecutive losses in which he'd allowed 13 runs in just 12.1 innings. His record stood at 8–12, his worst since he finished 11–17 in 1978, the year of his first no-hitter.

Worn down by a rough season and, at 33, looking near the end of the line, Forsch looked even less likely to throw a no-hitter than usual. But against an inconsistent Montreal Expos offense, Forsch wasn't just dominant—he was nearly perfect.

With Tim Raines and Andre Dawson, the Expos had one of the best outfields in baseball, and Gary Carter was dangerous behind the plate, but by September the seams

Lon Warneke and Importing No-Hitters

Lon Warneke is the kind of pitcher who was blessed, in the name-fertile 1930s, with a great real name and an even better nickname—"The Arkansas Hummingbird." He's also one of the few Cardinals stars to have made his name first as a Cub—at his best he won 20 games three times and won two games in Chicago's ill-fated 1935 World Series run. He's also the owner of the only Cardinals no-hitter thrown by a mercenary.

Acquired in trade for Gashouse Gang slugger Ripper Collins in 1937, Warneke had already won 74 games for the Cardinals when he made his historic start on August 30, 1941, with the Cardinals just a game back of the Dodgers for first in the National League.

With Elmer Riddle—15–2 at the time and the eventual ERA champion, along with owning an even cooler real name—opposite him on the mound, Warneke's six scoreless innings couldn't push the Cardinals ahead until errors behind Riddle undid him for good. Warneke, who allowed 25 of 28 batters faced to make contact, pushed through for the no-hitter and pushed the Cardinals into first place at the same time.

But it didn't last. The Cubs shut out Warneke and the Cardinals in his next start, and that night they fell a game out of first for good. And that is why the Cardinals never imported another no-hitter again. At least, maybe.

were starting to show elsewhere in their lineup—to face a seemingly gassed Forsch, the Expos brought out 21-year-old defensive specialist Angel Salazar, who was hitting well below the Mendoza line, at shortstop, and ageless utility man Chris Speier to give Tim Wallach the day off at third base.

It was a reasonable move, given Forsch's struggles and the imminent end of the season, but as it turned out the 12,457 fans at Busch Stadium—the 23,952 people who saw either of Forsch's no-hitters fall another 14,000 fans short of the Cardinals' average attendance in 2011—were about to see the best moment of that benighted season. Here was a Bob

Forsch who probably would have retired Babe Ruth as easily as Tim Wallach as easily as Chris Speier.

All that kept this Bob Forsch from the first perfect game in Cardinals history was, fittingly enough, something distinctly uncharacteristic of the control artist. With two out and nobody on in the second inning, Forsch, who hit a batter once every 10 starts over his 16-season career, plugged Carter. Things got weirder still after that—the normally steady Ken Oberkfell made an error on a routine groundball to put runners on first and third. To close out that deeply unconventional inning, it came down to Forsch, who struck out Salazar.

The St. Louis Browns and No-Hitters

The St. Louis Browns, the Cardinals' perennially beleaguered American League roommates, were as troubled by the no-hitter as they were by most everything else. In their 52 years as a franchise, they were no-hit eight times, one more than the Cardinals have managed in more than 130 years as a going concern.

They did punch back, for what it's worth, in their usual colorful way. Browns pitchers threw four no-hitters over that time period, beginning with Earl Hamilton in 1912—he allowed a run in the win, of course, one of 17 pitchers to do so since 1900—and ending with Bobo Holloman, who threw a no-hitter in the last year of the franchise's existence (and his first-ever start).

But the most impressive feat had to come on May 6 and 7, 1917, when rotation-mates Ernie Koob and Bob Groom tossed no-hitters on back-to-back days against the Chicago White Sox. It was an incredible moment, the only time it's happened in major league history, but it was also a Browns moment—that year Koob and Groom combined to finish 14–33.

No Hitters Thrown Against the Cardinals

Pitcher	Team	Date	Score
Adonis Terry	Brooklyn Grays	July 24, 1886	1–0
Christy Mathewson	New York Giants	July 15, 1901	5–0
Mal Eason	Brooklyn Superbas	July 20, 1906	2–0
Hod Eller	Cincinnati Reds	May 11, 1919	6–0
Don Cardwell	Chicago Cubs	May 15, 1960	4–0
Gaylord Perry	San Francisco Giants	September 17, 1968	1–0
Tom Seaver	Cincinnati Reds	June 16, 1978	4–0
Fernando Valenzuela	Los Angeles Dodgers	June 29, 1990	1–0

It was one of six strikeouts that night for Forsch—a season high. It was also the last time an Expo would reach base. After that odd rally, Forsch would be perfect, retiring 21 Expos in order.

Behind the Numbers

Ted Breitenstein, who in 1891 became the first Cardinals pitcher to throw a no-hitter, was remarkable in a number of ways—for one thing, he was just 21 years old. For another, he was St. Louis born and raised and locally famous for his amateur pitching. (No word at press time as to which high school he attended.)

But the most impressive part of Breitenstein's feat was the timing. Not only was it the first start of his career, it came on the last day of the season—and on the last day of operations for the American Association, which folded after the season.

In the fifth inning the Cardinals bats did their part; facing Steve Rogers, the defending ERA champion, they played a stereotypically perfect inning of Whiteyball. David Green led off with a walk, advanced to second on a groundout, and scored on Ozzie Smith's single; Ozzie advanced to second on the throw and third on Forsch's fly ball, leaving him in position to score on Lonnie Smith's double; Lonnie scored on Willie McGee's single, and the Cardinals had all the runs they'd need.

Forsch wouldn't face anything approaching a threat after that. The ledger after that second inning reads five strikeouts, three pop-ups, nine groundballs, and just four balls out of the infield.

For a player whose career was defined by his no-hitters, Bob Forsch never seemed to buy into the mystique. He wasn't a flamethrower with strikeout stuff, and he wasn't the owner of a wipeout breaking ball that was easier to take than swing at. He just threw the ball and had enough confidence in his gameplan to wait for the hitters to retire themselves. It's a great way to win 168 games, but it's difficult to imagine that strategy producing two no-hitters.

But Bob Forsch wasn't even thinking about the no-hitters, let alone spooked by the various jinxes that strand pitchers in mid-no-hitter on the end of the bench, alone in the dugout. Years later he gave the St. Louis *Post-Dispatch* this terse description of what it was like to throw one. "They felt like every other game until at the end you knew they weren't like any other game… Look, at that point, you're either going to do it or not. It won't make a difference if somebody talks about it."

Of course, it doesn't matter what difference it's made ever since—people won't ever stop talking about Bob Forsch's two no-hitters.

Behind the Numbers

On September 17, 1968, Gaylord Perry became the second man to no-hit the Cardinals in eight years when he outdueled Bob Gibson in the middle of his historic Year of the Pitcher run, but the pain didn't last too long for Cardinals fans—the next day Ray Washburn, on his way to a 2.26 ERA of his own, no-hit Perry's Giants to return the favor.

CHAPTER 9

BOB CARUTHERS LEADS THE LEAGUE IN ERA AND OPS IN CONSECUTIVE SEASONS

Career Pitching Records

The Cardinals have had some impressive hitting pitchers in their long history as a franchise. Dizzy Dean slapped singles and stole bases while leading the Gashouse Gang from the mound; Bob Gibson hit 24 home runs and drove in 144 for his own cause, wiping more than a tenth of his career runs allowed off the books. Bob Forsch won two Silver Slugger Awards to go with his two no-hitters, and, most famously, Rick Ankiel went from pitching prospect of the decade to slugging center fielder in five years flat.

But none of those feats quite compare to the one the Cardinals' original superstar managed in the far-off American Association of 1885. Just 21 years old, "Parisian" Bob Caruthers achieved an almost unheard-of double-crown, leading the league in wins and ERA one year and OPS, or on-base plus slugging, the next.

He was a one-of-a-kind player who had landed, almost ideally, on a one-of-a-kind club—the original St. Louis Browns, run by the eccentric beer baron

Chris Von der Ahe. A saloon owner who'd come into the baseball business almost by accident—he'd seen how much his patrons enjoyed the games and wagered they'd enjoy them even more while buying his beer—Von der Ahe was almost entirely mystified by the game itself, which didn't keep him from eventually running nearly all the Browns' baseball operations and briefly installing himself as manager.

Luckily for Von der Ahe and his team, the club was good enough to run itself by then. Led by player-manager Charles Comiskey and star outfielder Tip O'Neill on offense, the team also led the Association in ERA behind outstanding performances from Caruthers and veteran Dave Foutz, who combined to pitch an incredible 88 percent of the team's innings in 1885.

Caruthers' preternatural command arrived almost out of nowhere—his 3.3 strikeouts for every walk were among the best ratios in baseball—but his hitting wasn't quite attention-grabbing yet. He hit .225 with 20 walks, an impressive show for a pitcher or a shortstop but not enough to stand out in the kind of primordial baseball world in which he found himself.

While Caruthers was establishing himself as the premier pitching star of the AA, Von der Ahe was erecting an enormous

Remember When...

Tony La Russa was never averse to making his starting pitchers try new things—witness Kyle Lohse, pinch-runner and left fielder—but few pitchers were used more frequently on their day off than Jason Marquis. In 2006, Marquis was called on 13 times as a pinch-hitter; he got three hits in 10 official at-bats, including a double and a triple, and scored three times. As a pitcher that year he hit just .162.

statue of himself outside the original Sportsman's Park. Later, he took advantage of his pennant-winning team's good fortune by holding the first ever World's Series, between his Browns and what would eventually become the Chicago Cubs—the teams tied, starting a rivalry that has gone on uninterrupted ever since.

It was exactly the kind of atmosphere Caruthers, a 5'7" southern dandy of a pitcher, was made for. After 1885 he and teammate Doc Bushong conducted a novel salary dispute from across the ocean in France, which earned Parisian Bob his effete nickname. In 1886 his bat was considered valuable enough that St. Louis—managed at the time by Comiskey, a famous strategist alleged to have been the first man to play off the bag at first base—moved him into the outfield on days he wasn't pitching.

Comiskey may or may not have been the first guy to notice that standing on first base all afternoon wasn't the optimal way to play defense, but Caruthers rapidly earned him the genius tag. The days off protected Caruthers' arm—pitchers had been allowed to throw overhand just two years earlier—and the time in the outfield revealed that the Browns' ace pitcher was also one of the most dangerous hitters in baseball.

It's hard to draw comparisons across 100 years of baseball evolution, but Caruthers at his best must have looked something like Rickey Henderson at the plate and a right-handed Tom Glavine in what was then known as the pitcher's box. Undersized even for his time, Caruthers had excellent speed—in 1886 he hit 14 triples and stole 26 bases—but was even more impressive when he didn't swing. That year he walked 64 times in 382 plate appearances, finishing just out of the American Association lead behind players who'd appeared in 40 more games.

His command on the mound—his walks allowed per nine innings were consistently among the lowest in baseball—seemed to transfer directly to his style at the plate; he knew what he wanted to avoid as a pitcher, and he made sure the other pitcher had trouble avoiding it.

That plate discipline, combined with the havoc a speed merchant could wreak on the basepaths when outfield fences were more a suggestion than a rule, made him the most dangerous hitter in baseball. His on-base percentage of .448 led the American Association, while his .527 slugging percentage, courtesy of all those triples and inside-the-park home runs, put him fractions below league leader Dave Orr, who walked just 17 times all year.

Put together, his .974 OPS was 84 points higher than the league's next-best hitter, on par with what Stan Musial managed in 1948 or Albert Pujols in 2008. Meanwhile, in his reduced pitching workload, Caruthers won 30 games with an ERA of 2.32, good for fifth and second in the association, respectively.

It was a kind of dominance nobody in baseball history would quite be able to replicate—even Babe Ruth began to transition

Behind the Numbers

On-Base Plus Slugging, or OPS, has emerged as a popular stat in recent years thanks to the way it combines the ability to reach base with the ability to hit the ball for extra bases in one easy back-of-the-envelope calculation.

Top Cardinals Pitchers' Hitting Seasons by OPS (On-Base Plus Slugging)

Rank	Player	Year	PA	AVG	OBP	SLG	OPS
1.	Bob Caruthers	1886	382	.334	.448	.527	.974
2.	Curt Davis	1939	115	.381	.398	.457	.855
3.	Bob Forsch	1987	71	.298	.333	.509	.842
4.	Jack Stivetts	1890	243	.288	.337	.500	.837
5.	Bob Forsch	1975	88	.308	.341	.462	.803
6.	Pink Hawley	1893	103	.286	.369	.429	.798
7.	Bob Forsch	1980	89	.295	.313	.474	.787
8.	Jason Marquis	2005	91	.310	.326	.460	.786
9.	Bill Sherdel	1923	93	.337	.389	.398	.786
10.	Mike O'Neill	1902	139	.319	.333	.444	.778

away from pitching the same year he first led the American League in home runs. Caruthers himself was, like most pitchers at the time, only able to manage the blistering

Behind the Numbers

Every year since 1980 managers and coaches have voted for the Silver Slugger Award, presented by Hillerich & Bradsby—manufacturers of the Louisville Slugger bat—to the best hitter at each position in each league. The first year the award was presented, Cardinals won five of the nine National League trophies.

Albert Pujols' four wins at first base tie him for the most of any player—a fact that's even more impressive when considered with his Silver Slugger awards at third base and in the outfield.

workload for seven seasons before he broke down.

He wouldn't even last that long in St. Louis. Von der Ahe's mercurial relationship with his best player broke down after the Browns' embarrassing loss in the 1887 World's Series. Caruthers—a sharp and avid gambler and carouser—was given the blame, both as the team's star and the primary symbol of its loose, unserious personality. (Von der Ahe, who would later attempt to turn the team's home field into an amusement park with water flumes, an artificial lake, and a horse track in fair territory, was apparently unwilling to point the finger at himself.)

And so it was that the Browns, who were beginning a rapid descent that would nearly lead to the end of the Cardinals before they began, sold Caruthers to the Brooklyn Bridegrooms in 1887

Career Pitching Records

Category	Number	Pitcher (Years)
Most Games	554	Jesse Haines (1920–37)
Most Saves	217	Jason Isringhausen (2002–08)
Lowest ERA (minimum 500 innings)	2.46	Ed Karger (1906–08)
Most Games Started	482	Bob Gibson (1959–75)
Most Wins	251	Bob Gibson (1959–75)
Innings Pitched	3,884.1	Bob Gibson (1959–75)
Most Strikeouts	3,117	Bob Gibson (1959–75)
Most Shutouts	56	Bob Gibson (1959–75)
Complete Games	255	Bob Gibson (1959–75)
Winning Percentage	.719	Ice Box Chamberlain (1888–90)
Most Losses	174	Bob Gibson (1959–75)
Home Runs Allowed	257	Bob Gibson (1959–75)
Most Walks	1,336	Bob Gibson (1959–75)
Most Hit Batsmen	102	Bob Gibson (1959–75)
Most Wild Pitches	111	Jumbo McGinnis (1882–86)

for a sum of $8,250—$200,000 in 2011 dollars—just months after he'd gone 29–9 and hit .357.

In 1892, with Von der Ahe destitute and increasingly desperate to bring fans back to the ballpark, Parisian Bob returned to the Browns—by then members of the National League after the American Association's rapid collapse—for one final go-around. He was 28, but by modern standards his arm was closer to 39; his 2,828 innings pitched are just a few more than Bob Forsch pitched in 16 major league seasons. He went just 2–10, with an ERA of 5.84, in 16 brutal appearances.

But the bat was still there. Spending a full season in the outfield, Caruthers drew 86 walks and added eight triples. The arm was no longer willing, but the outfielder still knew exactly what pitchers didn't want. It was a volatile career in a more volatile time for baseball, but for a few seasons Bob Caruthers was as valuable as any player has ever been.

Career Pitching Records

Games Started

Rank	Pitcher	Games Started	Years
1.	Bob Gibson	482	1959–75
2.	Bob Forsch	401	1974–88
3.	Jesse Haines	386	1920–37
4.	Bill Doak	320	1913–24, 1929
5.	Bill Sherdel	243	1918–30, 1932
6.	Harry Brecheen	224	1940, 1943–52
7.	Ted Breitenstein	222	1891–96, 1901
8.	Slim Sallee	212	1908–16
9.	Larry Jackson	209	1955–62
10.	Matt Morris	206	1997–2005

Career Wins

Rank	Pitcher	Wins	Years
1.	Bob Gibson	251	1959–75
2.	Jesse Haines	210	1920–37
3.	Bob Forsch	163	1974–88
4.	Bill Sherdel	153	1918–30, 1932
5.	Bill Doak	144	1913–24, 1929
6.	Dizzy Dean	134	1930–37
7.	Harry Brecheen	128	1940, 1943–52
8.	Dave Foutz	114	1884–87
9.	Silver King	112	1887–89
10.	Bob Caruthers	108	1884–87, 1892

Career Losses

Rank	Pitcher	Losses	Years
1.	Bob Gibson	174	1959–75
2.	Jesse Haines	158	1920–37
3.	Bill Doak	136	1913–24, 1929
4.	Bill Sherdel	131	1918–30, 1932
5.	Bob Forsch	127	1974–88
6.	Ted Breitenstein	125	1891–96, 1901
7.	Slim Sallee	107	1908–16
8.	Larry Jackson	86	1955–62
9.	Bob Harmon	81	1909–13
10.	Harry Brecheen	79	1940, 1943–52

Career Pitching Records

Complete Games

Rank	Pitcher	Complete Games	Years
1.	Bob Gibson	255	1959–75
2.	Jesse Haines	208	1920–37
3.	Ted Breitenstein	198	1891–96, 1901
4.	Dave Foutz	156	1884–87
5.	Silver King	154	1887–89
6.	Bob Caruthers	151	1884–87, 1892
7.	Jumbo McGinnis	145	1882–86
8.	Bill Doak	144	1913–24, 1929
	Bill Sherdel		1918–30, 1932
10.	Dizzy Dean	141	1930–37

Career Innings Pitched

Rank	Pitcher	Innings Pitched	Years
1.	Bob Gibson	3,884.1	1959–75
2.	Jesse Haines	3,203.2	1920–37
3.	Bob Forsch	2,658.2	1974–88
4.	Bill Sherdel	2,450.2	1918–30, 1932
5.	Bill Doak	2,387.0	1913–24, 1929
6.	Ted Breitenstein	1,934.1	1891–96, 1901
7.	Slim Sallee	1,905.1	1908–16
8.	Harry Brecheen	1,790.1	1940, 1943–52
9.	Dizzy Dean	1,737.1	1930–37
10.	Larry Jackson	1,672.1	1955–62

Home Runs Allowed

Rank	Pitcher	Home Runs Allowed	Years
1.	Bob Gibson	257	1959–75
2.	Bob Forsch	204	1974–88
3.	Jesse Haines	165	1920–37
4.	Larry Jackson	152	1955–62
5.	Matt Morris	129	1997–2005
6.	Bill Sherdel	126	1918–30, 1932
7.	Ray Sadecki	125	1960–66, 1975
8.	Gerry Staley	114	1947–54
9.	Harry Brecheen	110	1940, 1943–52
	Ernie Broglio		1959–64

Career Pitching Records

Career Strikeouts

Rank	Pitcher	Strikeouts	Years
1.	Bob Gibson	3,117	1959–75
2.	Dizzy Dean	1,095	1930–37
3.	Bob Forsch	1,079	1974–88
4.	Chris Carpenter	1,073	2004–11
5.	Matt Morris	986	1997–2005
6.	Jesse Haines	979	1920–37
7.	Steve Carlton	951	1965–71
8.	Bill Doak	938	1913–24, 1929
9.	Larry Jackson	899	1955–62
10.	Harry Brecheen	857	1940, 1943–52

Career Walks Allowed

Rank	Pitcher	Walks	Years
1.	Bob Gibson	1,336	1959–75
2.	Jesse Haines	870	1920–37
3.	Ted Breitenstein	843	1891–96, 1901
4.	Bob Forsch	780	1974–88
5.	Bill Doak	740	1913–24, 1929
6.	Bill Hallahan	648	1925–26, 1929–36
7.	Bill Sherdel	595	1918–30, 1932
8.	Bob Harmon	594	1909–13
9.	Vinegar Bend Mizell	568	1952–53, 1956–60
10.	Max Lanier	524	1938–46, 1949–51

Most Home Runs Hit by Cardinals Pitchers

Rank	Pitcher	Home Runs	Years
1.	Bob Gibson	24	1959–75
2.	Jack Stivetts	14	1889–91
3.	Bob Forsch	12	1974–88
4.	Bill Sherdel	9	1918–32
5.	Dizzy Dean	8	1930–37

Redbird Reference

Rick Ankiel

By 2007 even Cardinals fans who were willing to break the taboo on mentioning a pitcher's no-hitter had stopped talking out loud about Rick Ankiel. At 27 years old, he'd already put together one of the best rookie seasons a Cardinals pitcher ever had, melted down multiple times on national television, made a comeback that was an unmitigated success, retired permanently from pitching, and suffered season-ending injuries as a pitcher and an outfielder.

But the fans who watched the minor leagues couldn't keep themselves from whispering. Ankiel had played half a season in the outfield in 2005, hitting 21 home runs in 85 games, before a knee injury in 2006 cost him an entire season of work, but the Cardinals pushed him all the way to Memphis to start the 2007 season, which is when the Rick Ankiel legend began adding pages after a long layoff.

When he was a 20-year-old left-hander with a mid-90s fastball and an even better curveball, it had been a funny footnote for broadcasters in the middle of 10-strikeout games: Rick Ankiel had more power than most of the Cardinals' position players. In 1997, at the World Junior Championships, his .387 batting average had tied Matt Holliday for tops on Team USA. In 2000, as a 20-year-old player in the major leagues who got to play once every five games, he hit .250.

It was something to see a pitcher swing as hard—and get as frustrated when he struck out—as Mark McGwire or Jim Edmonds, but it was nothing compared to the pitching. Whatever he did at the plate that year couldn't compete. On April 20 he went 3–3 with a home run but also pitched five scoreless innings. On July 21 he went 2–3 with a walk and an RBI and, while he was at it, struck out 11 Houston Astros in seven innings. (In the eighth Tony La Russa still called for a pinch hitter—Craig Paquette, who would finish with a batting average five points lower than Ankiel's.)

All through the regular season his hitting was just a trivia question compared to his pitching, which began to justify the Sandy Koufax comparisons that had floated up through the minor leagues. That September he struck out 40 batters against just 11 walks in 32⅔ innings, going 3–0 with an ERA of 1.65. And after the playoffs—well, no one remembers that amid the 11 walks and nine wild pitches, he went 0–1 in his only at-bat in the NLDS.

In 2001, after it became clear the 10 pitches he'd thrown to the backstop in his two playoff starts were more than a nerve-wracking aberration, the power went from footnote to sideshow: Sent down to rookie ball, where he was still younger than many of his teammates, he made 14 starts, played 27 times as the Johnson City Cardinals' designated hitter, and had one of the most overwhelming seasons in the history of baseball.

Rick Ankiel in Rookie Ball

G	AB	R	H	2B	3B	HR	RBI	AVG	OBP	SLG
41	105	21	30	7	0	10	35	.286	.364	.638

W	L	ERA	GS	IP	R	ER	HR	BB	SO	K:BB
5	3	1.33	14	87.2	20	13	1	18	158	8.78

His .638 slugging percentage led all players with at least 20 games, and his 158 strikeouts—an astounding 16.2 per nine innings against just 18 walks—were 69 more than the pitcher who finished number two in the Appalachian League. In one game he struck out 14 batters without allowing a walk; the next day, taking the number-three slot in the batting order, he homered.

The understated verdict, according to Yadier Molina, then his 19-year-old personal catcher: "He's improved a great deal. He's ready to go back."

They were video-game numbers and a frightening reminder of just how talented Ankiel was, but each new season the home runs—they kept coming—were just a way to pass the time between worrying setbacks and triumphant returns.

It wasn't until 2005, where a brief and sudden setback at spring training spelled the end of his pitching career, that fans finally took stock of Rick Ankiel the hitter. Sent in to man right and later center field, his outfield arm was obviously never in doubt; at the plate he was still a hyper-talented high schooler, overmatched by veteran pitchers but able to pull any fastball over the fence.

Now 25 and distinctly old for the low minors, he slugged his way to the AA Texas League, popping 21 home runs and 17 doubles across a half-season in the minor leagues. In 2006 he was a long shot for a spot on the major league bench when a severe knee injury ended his season before it began. As he rehabbed, out of the public eye again, it seemed like he would never get the chance to make his long-awaited comeback, and Cardinals fans who had gotten their hopes up six times before found it best to ignore his seventh comeback season, this one coming as AAA Memphis' starting right fielder.

No more than a month passed before his progress became impossible to ignore. Ankiel certainly didn't look like a polished outfielder—he struck out in a quarter of his at-bats and hardly ever walked—but he looked like a real one, manning right field so well that some suggested he could play center. After a slow start his batting average began to climb, and the home runs finally looked like something other than a sideshow—they looked like his ticket to the major leagues.

Suddenly he was hitting a lot of them; suddenly he was leading the Pacific Coast League in home runs with 32 and slugging a healthy .568 besides.

And not so suddenly the St. Louis Cardinals found themselves out of outfielders. A year after their improbable World Series victory, the Cardinals had to deal with the hangover—an aging Jim Edmonds, a defensively challenged Chris Duncan, and Juan Encarnacion as himself. When Scott Spiezio left the team on August 9, the Cardinals had no other option. Rick Ankiel would be given one last chance at a comeback.

That night saw Busch Stadium giddier and more nervous than it had been since that NLDS game in 2000 when the Rick Ankiel story had begun. Fans whispered like they had when Ankiel had sailed fastballs over Carlos Hernandez's head. Would he be able to handle it? Was he really an outfielder?

That Thursday night 42,848 in attendance at Busch Stadium gave Rick Ankiel one more standing ovation as he jogged into right field. The Cardinals were six games under .500, but the ovation rolled across the crowd like it was opening night of the playoffs. It came again at the top of the inning when Ankiel caught a routine fly ball behind Joel Pineiro, and again in the bottom of the first when he popped up weakly to shortstop. It came once more, nervously, when he struck out in the third and the fifth.

The fans at Busch Stadium had seen Rick Ankiel come back to the mound in April 2001 supposedly cured of his control problems. They'd heard him rehab in 2002 and 2003 and watched him look like the old Rick Ankiel in 2004 only to retire. They'd waited through a knee injury and a year and a half spent learning the outfield on the job.

They got up one more time in the seventh inning, the Cardinals clinging to a 2–0 lead with their season on the line, and gave Rick Ankiel a standing ovation. And with So Taguchi and Adam Kennedy on base and two men out, Ankiel pulled a 2–1 pitch from Doug Brocail 383' into the stands in right field.

There was cheering. There was a curtain call so long that the rest of the 5–0 win seemed like anticlimax. And nearly seven years after the best pitching prospect of his generation lost the ability to pitch for good, he circled the bases and went into the box score as ANKIEL, RF, just another slugger on the St. Louis Cardinals.

Cardinals Silver Slugger Award Winners

Year	Player	Position	Year	Player	Position
1980	Bob Forsch	Pitcher	2001	Albert Pujols	Third Base
	Ted Simmons	Catcher	2002	Edgar Renteria	Shortstop
	Keith Hernandez	First Base	2003	Edgar Renteria	Shortstop
	Garry Templeton	Shortstop		Albert Pujols	Outfield
	George Hendrick	Outfield	2004	Albert Pujols	First Base
1983	George Hendrick	First Base		Jim Edmonds	Outfield
1985	Jack Clark	First Base	2005	Jason Marquis	Pitcher
	Willie McGee	Outfield	2008	Albert Pujols	First Base
1987	Bob Forsch	Pitcher		Ryan Ludwick	Outfield
	Jack Clark	First Base	2009	Albert Pujols	First Base
	Ozzie Smith	Shortstop	2010	Albert Pujols	First Base
1998	Mark McGwire	First Base		Matt Holliday	Outfield
2000	Edgar Renteria	Shortstop			

Chapter 10

Bruce Sutter Saves the Cardinals' First World Series Since 1967

Relief Records

In the history of the infamous rivalry between the Cardinals and the Chicago Cubs—going back more than a century—very few players have managed success in both cities. The most famous story of a player going from Chicago to St. Louis, the one about Lou Brock, is characterized when told inside Busch Stadium as a theft, just another shot fired in the teams' long list of acrimonious dealings.

Bruce Sutter is different. He arrived in St. Louis already an All-Star closer—a Cy Young Award winner as Wrigley's fire chief in 1979—and he came over in exchange for Ken Reitz, one of the most popular figures in the Cardinals' lost decade, and Leon Durham, who'd later star for the Cubs.

It was one of the many moves that saw Whitey Herzog remake a team that had been stuck in the middle of the National League East for years into a World Series contender, and when Game 7 of the 1982 World Series rolled around, Sutter became a Cardinal for all time when he found himself on the mound with his new team's first championship since 1967 in the balance.

It was a long way from where he'd begun his career as a struggling reliever at the very edges of the Cubs' minor league system with a bum arm and no out pitch.

That's where the Bruce Sutter story starts, in St. Louis or Chicago or at Cooperstown—nearly out of baseball, with nothing to go on but a pitch no one had ever heard of. After elbow surgery robbed him of his old fastball velocity, the Cubs' roving pitching instructor, Fred Martin, convinced the stalled minor leaguer to try a pitch he'd begun evangelizing called the split-fingered fastball. Closely resembling the forkball with its wide grip, the splitter was thrown like a fastball and broke sharply—where most forkball adherents used the pitch as a change of pace, the modified version dove into the ground despite its straight release, and it became Sutter's main attraction.

The splitter might just be a glorified forkball or it might not, but it imparts an attitude, one Sutter would eventually pass down to a generation of closers that rode one brilliant pitch to unhittable success. A forkball confuses batters, befuddles them, baffles them—a splitter mows them down.

And after a mediocre 1973 run in Quincy, Illinois—five

Redbird Reference

Jason Isringhausen

Nobody personified the razor's-edge life of the closer quite like Jason Isringhausen, both in the game and out of it. The best pitching prospect in baseball in 1995, Isringhausen suffered from overuse and ever-stranger health problems—he dealt with everything from tuberculosis to a wrist he broke against an errant trash can—and, after multiple major surgeries, was on the fringes of baseball when he was traded to Oakland in 1999.

Then, all of a sudden, he was a closer, and a good one. He was just as unpredictable on the field; he could be simultaneously unhittable and completely out of control, and in long stretches of his career he abandoned pitches when they didn't suit him.

When things were working, though, Isringhausen was among the top closers in baseball. Arriving in St. Louis with a mid-90s fastball, he was able to adjust to declining velocity by adopting a cutter—the Dave Duncan special—that he'd hammer the outside corner with until batters surrendered and finally swung at it. And always lurking in the back of the hitter's mind was a knuckle-curveball that was almost too good—so sharp that Isringhausen could rarely keep it out of the dirt.

"Izzy" didn't do anything good for Cardinals fans' blood pressure during his seven years as closer, but his 217 saves proved him worthwhile in the end, no matter how dramatic they usually were.

hours from Chicago but about as far from the major leagues as a pitcher can get—Sutter began mowing them down, first with two dominant seasons in the minor leagues and then, by 1976, with a series of equally dominant seasons in the majors. It was a long way from being signed as a minor league free agent in 1971.

By the time he arrived in St. Louis, though, he and his incredible pitch were a known quantity, one acquired for two well-regarded regulars. Closers in 1982 hadn't quite gotten the full Tony La Russa treatment, so he was more of a regular himself than it might seem at first glance. Sutter had pitched 100 innings in a season three times already, picking up 15 two-inning saves in 1980 and 13 more (out of 25 total) in 1981, his first year under Whitey Herzog.

From the start of the season it was clear 1982 was nothing different. Nine of Sutter's first 10 appearances began in the eighth inning, and in four two-inning appearances that April he'd hardly been touched.

The Cardinals' reliance on their fireman burned them early. After a hot start he blew four games in rapid succession in June as the Cardinals rapidly fell from five games up to out of first place in the NL East. Sutter was in just as much trouble—after allowing seven earned runs in two

Unbreakable?

Bruce Sutter is one of two pitchers ever to win four National League Relief Man Awards—three with the Cardinals and one, during his Cy Young season of 1979, with the Cubs. Lee Smith, who won the award in each of his two full years with the club, won the American League award in 1994 with the Baltimore Orioles (formerly the St. Louis Browns, if you'd like to stretch things).

appearances against the Mets his ERA climbed to 4.96, with 8.96 on the month.

But Herzog never stopped going back to the well. The next day Sutter went two scoreless innings to earn a late win against the third-place Phillies, and he earned his 16th and 17th saves in a doubleheader on June 26.

The Cardinals and Sutter held steady through July, but it was his performance down the stretch that separated them from the rest of the league. In the last two months of the season Sutter pitched 39 innings, recorded 15 saves with an ERA of 1.37, and wiped out any lingering doubts as to the identity of the most dominant closer in the National League. In his last 14 innings he didn't allow an earned run and secured the league lead in saves for his fourth consecutive season.

He also secured his first ever postseason berth, and the Cardinals' first since 1968. Sutter, ready to be brought in at any moment, was perfectly suited for the role, and there are few more characteristic moments in his career than the four scoreless innings he pitched across back-to-back days to help win the Cardinals' NLCS matchup against the Atlanta Braves.

Sutter's seven World Series innings were less perfect, but his Game 7 appearance on October 20 was prototypical Bruce Sutter. Coming into the game in the eighth inning, the Cardinals ahead by a single run, Sutter came in and dealt with the top of the Brewers' order as though it were a mid-May game with the 100-loss Reds. Paul Molitor grounded out to Ozzie Smith at short, Robin Yount struck out swinging, and Cecil Cooper grounded out to second.

The Cardinals rewarded him in the bottom of the inning with more runs than he'd need—Lonnie Smith hit a ground-rule double down the right-field line, and Darrell Porter and Steve Braun singled in back-to-back at-bats to put the Cardinals up three runs with just three outs separating them from their ninth world championship.

Sutter took 17 pitches and a minimum of fuss. Ted Simmons, who'd been traded controversially just the year before, grounded right

Behind the Numbers

The Rolaids Relief Man Award is one of the few awards in baseball determined by a strict formula. Created in 1976, the current formula involves adding up the following point values: three points for each save; two points for each win; four points for each "tough save," earned with the tying run on base. Two points are then deducted for each loss and blown save.

back to him; Ben Oglivie grounded out right behind him. Gorman Thomas took a little more doing, but after fouling off three pitches he obliged the photographers by striking out swinging on a beautiful fastball. Porter's leap into the air—and then into Sutter's arms—would be the last good late-inning news the Cardinals would get in the postseason for almost 25 years.

It was Sutter's last trip to the postseason, too. He had just one more full season in that temperamental right arm.

Pitching coaches will never quite agree on just how hard the splitter is on a pitcher's arm, but the whispers were finally proven true in 1985 when Sutter, a year after signing a $10 millon deal with the Atlanta Braves, succumbed to the shoulder problems that would end his career after just 661 appearances and 1,042 innings. Given current thought on pitcher usage patterns, it's perhaps more likely that the 122 innings he pitched in his remarkable 1984 season, which earned him his fourth Top 10 MVP finish, had something to do with it.

But Sutter's influence on baseball—both during his career and after it was over—proved difficult to measure with innings pitched alone. After 13 years of votes, in which his role as closer and his status as the Johnny Appleseed of the split-fingered fastball only loomed larger in baseball history, Sutter was elected to the Hall of Fame in 2006, just the fourth relief pitcher in baseball history to earn that honor.

No member had pitched fewer innings or earned their plaque without ever having made a major league start, but by then nobody was surprised to see Bruce Sutter doing something new and unexpected.

That July in Cooperstown, as his plaque was unveiled—complete with Cardinals cap—Sutter told his improbable story one more time. He talked about going from a "suspect" to a prospect with one new pitch; he talked about the feeling of playing baseball in St. Louis, of walking onto the field as cheers of "Bruuuuce!" fell dissonantly onto the field.

But people will always talk about Sutter's split-fingered

Redbird Reference
Todd Worrell

Few positions in baseball offer the manager as much room for superstition as the closer, and one of the most important superstitions for closers is that being an experienced veteran is vitally important for dealing with high-pressure situations—until it isn't. Todd Worrell is a perfect example. Joining the Cardinals in September 1985, after a season spent juggling successors to the departed Bruce Sutter, Worrell had five saves and 21 innings to his name when the Cardinals called on him for 11 innings in their World Series run that same year.

Worrell put together four more seasons as an excellent closer after that postseason, but his career almost ended as abruptly as it began when he suffered elbow and shoulder injuries in rapid succession following the 1989 season. Nearly three years later Worrell returned to the Cardinals and looked, startlingly, as good as he had before—working now as Lee Smith's set-up man, Worrell set the Cardinals' all-time saves record and moved on to the Los Angeles Dodgers, where he led Major League Baseball in saves in 1996.

fastball, the most disruptive pitch of the 1980s. Sutter himself put it best: "Without it," he said, after three shoulder surgeries, "I would've been, at best, a Double-A player. If they told me it would hurt my arm if I threw it, I'd do it all over again."

THE RYNE SANDBERG GAME

It's a good thing for Sutter that he introduced the world to a new pitch and became one of the greatest relief pitchers of all time, because if he hadn't done it he might still be famous today, for one terrible reason: the Ryne Sandberg Game.

On June 23, 1984, in the midst of perhaps the best season of his career, Sutter came in for a two-plus-innings save attempt against the Cubs, who at 37–31 were surprise contenders as summer dawned. His ERA was just 1.19, and if anyone seemed able to protect the Cardinals' fragile 9–8 lead it was the National League's best closer, who retired the first batter he saw to get the Cardinals out of trouble in the seventh.

They'd gotten into trouble, at least in part, thanks to Ryne Sandberg, the Cubs' young second baseman, who was in the midst of a breakout season. He'd driven in four runs already and lurked four batters away in the second spot in the Cubs' order.

Sutter got through the bottom of the eighth in order, but when the Cardinals failed to make something of their ninth inning rally, Sandberg led off the bottom of the inning with a booming home run into the Wrigley Field bleachers, tying the game against an old Cubs hero.

Sutter was rattled but not beaten—he got out of a first-and-third jam with a ground ball to short, and when Willie McGee completed his cycle with an RBI double off Lee Smith in the top of the 10th, it became clear Sutter would have another chance.

Unfortunately, that chance came against Ryne Sandberg with a runner on first base and two out. Sandberg homered again, driving in his sixth and seventh runs, and the Cubs went on to win in 11 innings, keying a run that brought Sandberg the MVP trophy and Chicago its first postseason appearance since 1945.

In general, it's never good to be the pitcher in a game known to history for an opposing batter. But Sutter got over it, at least eventually—in his Hall of Fame induction speech, he made sure to talk about learning important lessons. "[Be] on time… practice things until they become instinctive, and never make the same mistake twice." He was talking about lessons he'd learned from his high school coaches, but he made sure to note that he'd kept learning that last one. "Mr. Sandberg," he conceded, "helped me with that."

Cardinals Relief Man Award Winners

Year	Pitcher	ERA	Record	Saves
1981	Bruce Sutter	2.62	3–5	25
1982	Bruce Sutter	2.90	9–8	36
1984	Bruce Sutter	1.54	5–7	45
1986	Todd Worrell	2.08	9–10	36
1991	Lee Smith	2.34	6–3	47
1992	Lee Smith	3.12	4–9	43
1995	Tom Henke	1.82	1–1	36

Career Saves

Rank	Pitcher	Saves	Years
1.	Jason Isringhausen	217	2002–08
2.	Lee Smith	160	1990–93
3,	Todd Worrell	129	1985–89, 1992
4.	Bruce Sutter	127	1981 84
5.	Ryan Franklin	84	2007–11
6.	Dennis Eckersley	66	1996–97
7.	Lindy McDaniel	64	1955 62
8.	Al Brazle	60	1943, 1946–54
	Joe Hoerner		1966–69
10.	Al Hrabosky	59	1970 77

Saves in a Single Season

Rank	Pitcher	Saves	Year
1.	Lee Smith	47	1991
	Jason Isringhausen		2004
3.	Bruce Sutter	45	1984
4.	Lee Smith	43	1992
	Lee Smith		1993
6.	Jason Isringhausen	39	2005
7.	Ryan Franklin	38	2009
8.	Bruce Sutter	36	1982
	Todd Worrell		1986
	Tom Henke		1995
	Dennis Eckersley		1997

Career Games Pitched

Rank	Pitcher	Games	Years
1.	Jesse Haines	554	1920–37
2.	Bob Gibson	528	1959–75
3.	Bill Sherdel	465	1918–30, 1932
4.	Bob Forsch	455	1974–88
5.	Al Brazle	441	1943, 1946–54
6.	Jason Isringhausen	401	2002–08
7.	Bill Doak	376	1914–24, 1929
8.	Todd Worrell	348	1985–89, 1992
9.	Lindy McDaniel	336	1955–62
10.	Larry Jackson	330	1955–62

Games Pitched in a Single Season

Rank	Pitcher	Games	Year
1.	Steve Kline	89	2001
2.	Ray King	86	2004
3.	Steve Kline	78	2003
	Jason Motte		2011
5.	Mike Perez	77	1992
	Julian Tavarez		2004
	Ray King		2005
8.	Russ Springer	76	2007
9.	Todd Worrell	75	1987
	Dennys Reyes		2009

Career Games Finished

Rank	Pitcher	Games Finished	Years
1.	Jason Isringhausen	332	2002–08
2.	Todd Worrell	232	1985–89, 1992
3.	Lee Smith	209	1990–93
4.	Bruce Sutter	203	1981–84
5.	Lindy McDaniel	188	1955–62
6.	Al Hrabosky	182	1970–77
7.	Al Brazle	178	1943, 1946–54
8.	Ryan Franklin	161	2007–11
9.	Bill Sherdel	152	1918–30, 1932
10.	Joe Hoerner	137	1966–69

CHAPTER 11

SILVER KING WINS 45 GAMES
(And Other Unbreakable Cardinals Records)

Some Cardinal could theoretically win more games than Bob Gibson's 251. They could even rap more base hits than Stan Musial's 3,630 and make a run at Jim Bottomley's sacrifice bunt record (somebody has to have it) while they're at it. Ed Karger's ERA (2.46, just ahead of John Tudor), Gibby's strikeouts (3,117), and Jason Isringhausen's saves (217) could all go down before this copy of *The Ultimate Cardinals Record Book* decomposes in some post-apocalyptic used book store. But nobody in any future Busch Stadium will ever win more games in a season than Silver King's 45.

They'd be lucky to do it in any two consecutive seasons. Such is baseball history. Some records are difficult to break because a player was so good, but a different subset is impossible to break because baseball was unrecognizable when it was first set.

Silver King, a teenage prodigy who jumped from the dissolving Kansas City Cowboys of the National League to the St. Louis Browns

before the 1887 season, went 32–12 in his first full year with the club, sharing pitching duties with veteran Dave Foutz (25–12) and superstar pitcher-outfielder Bob Caruthers (29–9). In 2011 a 19-year-old with great stuff would be on strict pitch counts; in 1887 the sidearmer led the pennant-winning Browns with 390 innings.

King was so good that the Browns' eccentric owner, Chris von der Ahe, sold Caruthers to Brooklyn and let Foutz—who'd won 41 games just the year before—follow him there. With two even younger pitchers as his only help in the rotation, King made 64 of the team's 137 starts that year, going 45–20 and leading the American Association in wins, games, shutouts, innings pitched (584⅔), and ERA (1.63.)

He was, predictably, finished by the time he was 24 years old.

You would recognize what Silver King played as baseball, but not right away. A base on balls wouldn't come after four pitches out of the strike zone for another year; catchers weren't allowed to wear mitts, and they'd just begun to wear chest protectors. And 1887 was the first year a hitter was no longer allowed to call for a high or a low pitch. The debate over new-fangled statistics was played out between the old guard's Runs per Inning, which had dominated the box scores of the 1860s, and

Behind the Numbers

The Gold Glove Awards, presented by Rawlings, have been given since 1957 to the best defensive players at each position, as voted by managers and coaches in each league. The coaches are often derided for some of their more esoteric selections—Rafael Palmeiro once won a Gold Glove at first base despite playing just 28 games there—but it's difficult to criticize them for selecting Ozzie Smith 13 consecutive times, including 11 as a Cardinal.

batting average, which emerged along with the National League.

There was probably no outfield fence at your local ballpark, and for his part Silver King pitched in a "crossfire" motion out of something called a pitcher's box, 50' away from the hitter. (King's motion was the subject of much debate—he started from one edge of the box and swept all the way to the other side before delivering the ball sidearm.)

That, then, is how you win 45 games and pitch 584 innings in a season. At 60'6", with pitchers on strict pitch counts from the moment they leave aluminum bats behind and begin drawing paychecks, even Chris Carpenter would find it difficult to convince his pitching coach to leave him in. Here are some other players who've been helped to their slice of immortality by changes in rules and run-scoring:

1. Tip O'Neill's .492 batting average. The only record in Cardinals history even more defined by its context than Silver King, Tip O'Neill managed to hit .492—the highest single-season batting average ever—by hitting .435 at the right moment in history.

The year 1887 was the only year in major league history when a walk was counted as a base hit, and O'Neill, already one of the most dangerous hitters in the American Association, put together what was far and away the best season of his career that year, hitting what we would recognize as .435 and leading the league in runs scored (167), hits (225), doubles (52), triples (19), home runs (14), and RBIs (123.)

Under the rules of that one season, however, O'Neill just missed being the only player in major league history to bat above .500. If you're not willing to give the AA's 1887 braintrust that much credit, it's all academic, anyway. O'Neill's .435 average is itself 11 points higher than Rogers Hornsby's best season.

And that's not even taking into account his second career as Speaker of the House in the 1980s.

2. Mark McGwire's 70 home runs. It could be that the recent decline in home run totals is just a historical blip, but less than 20 years after McGwire's record-breaking season it seems impossible to imagine a player who could hit a home run every seven times the pitcher was brave enough to throw to him.

The Cardinals have had some great home run hitters—Albert Pujols, Johnny Mize, Rogers Hornsby—but Mark McGwire is still the only Cardinal ever to hit 70, 60, or 50 home runs in a single season.

Only one other hitter has even come close—Pujols owns the four highest totals after McGwire, but he missed joining the 50-home-run club by a single circuit clout in 2006.

3. Ozzie Smith's 11 consecutive Gold Gloves. Playing defense is a young man's game. Research suggests that if hitters peak sometimes around 27, defensive brilliance is something for teenagers and early-twentysomethings who have fresh arms and legs that no amount of veteran smarts can make up.

That's true for most shortstops, but it wasn't for Ozzie Smith, who arrived in St. Louis a 27-year-old with two Gold Gloves and proceeded to win the next 11—and deservedly so. According to some advanced statistics, Smith had his best defensive season in 1989 when he was 34 years old. That's why no Cardinal is likely to match his 11 consecutive Gold

Cardinals Gold Glove Award Winners

Year	Player	Position	Year	Player	Position
1958	Ken Boyer	Third Base	1985	Ozzie Smith	Shortstop
1959	Ken Boyer	Third Base		Willie McGee	Outfield
1960	Bill White	First Base	1986	Ozzie Smith	Shortstop
	Ken Boyer	Third Base		Willie McGee	Outfield
1961	Bill White	First Base	1987	Terry Pendleton	Third Base
	Ken Boyer	Third Base		Ozzie Smith	Shortstop
1962	Bobby Shantz	Pitcher	1988	Ozzie Smith	Shortstop
	Bill White	First Base	1989	Terry Pendleton	Third Base
1963	Bobby Shantz	Pitcher		Ozzie Smith	Shortstop
	Bill White	First Base	1990	Ozzie Smith	Shortstop
	Ken Boyer	Third Base	1991	Tom Pagnozzi	Catcher
	Curt Flood	Outfield		Ozzie Smith	Shortstop
1964	Bobby Shantz	Pitcher	1992	Tom Pagnozzi	Catcher
	Bill White	First Base		Ozzie Smith	Shortstop
1965	Bob Gibson	Pitcher	1994	Tom Pagnozzi	Catcher
	Bill White	First Base	2000	Mike Matheny	Catcher
	Curt Flood	Outfield		Jim Edmonds	Outfield
1966	Bob Gibson	Pitcher	2001	Fernando Vina	Second Base
	Curt Flood	Outfield		Jim Edmonds	Outfield
1967	Bob Gibson	Pitcher	2002	Fernando Vina	Second Base
	Curt Flood	Outfield		Scott Rolen	Third Base
1968	Bob Gibson	Pitcher		Jim Edmonds	Outfield
	Dal Maxvill	Shortstop	2003	Mike Matheny	Catcher
	Curt Flood	Outfield		Scott Rolen	Third Base
1969	Bob Gibson	Pitcher		Edgar Renteria	Shortstop
	Curt Flood	Outfield		Jim Edmonds	Outfield
1970	Bob Gibson	Pitcher	2004	Mike Matheny	Catcher
1971	Bob Gibson	Pitcher		Scott Rolen	Third Base
1972	Bob Gibson	Pitcher		Jim Edmonds	Outfield
1973	Bob Gibson	Pitcher	2005	Jim Edmonds	Outfield
1975	Ken Reitz	Third Base	2006	Albert Pujols	First Base
1978	Keith Hernandez	First Base		Scott Rolen	Third Base
1979	Keith Hernandez	First Base	2008	Yadier Molina	Catcher
1980	Keith Hernandez	First Base	2009	Adam Wainwright	Pitcher
1981	Keith Hernandez	First Base		Yadier Molina	Catcher
1982	Keith Hernandez	First Base	2010	Yadier Molina	Catcher
	Ozzie Smith	Shortstop		Albert Pujols	First Base
1983	Ozzie Smith	Shortstop	2011	Yadier Molina	Catcher
	Willie McGee	Outfield			
1984	Joaquin Andujar	Pitcher			
	Ozzie Smith	Shortstop			

Gloves, especially at the most demanding defensive position of all.

4. Stan Musial's 177 triples. If you really want to know the kind of player Stan Musial was, you can look at nearly everything he did on a baseball field. All of it paints a picture of a tireless worker and a flawless athlete. But nothing says quite so much in so little space as Musial's 177 triples. The Man

led the National League five times in that category, picking up 20 in a season twice, and he did it despite never being known for his quickness.

He just hit the ball hard and he ran. Without line-drive hitters like that, hustle like that, and continuity like that—Musial hit 10 triples in 1942, two triples in 1963, and 165 in between—it's impossible to imagine a Cardinal

Redbird Reference
Brian Jordan

Every year hundreds of major league draft picks are two-sport athletes. Every several years one of those athletes is good enough that he moves from one sport to another. But of those few, even fewer do what Brian Jordan did. The Cardinals outfielder played both baseball and football at the same time, toiling in the minor leagues in the summer while playing defensive back for the Atlanta Falcons in the NFL.

In 1988, when the Cardinals took him 30th overall in the MLB Draft, Jordan was a much better prospect in baseball than in football. Eventually he went in the seventh round of the 1989 NFL Draft, going to the Buffalo Bills at the verge of Mr. Irrelevancy. Most players might have taken his subsequent release in stride and concentrated on baseball year-round. Instead, Jordan made the Atlanta Falcons and developed into an All-Pro defensive back, leading the Falcons in tackles his final season and earning an alternate selection to the Pro Bowl.

Meanwhile, his baseball career had begun to stagnate. At 24 the former first-rounder hit just .264 with four home runs in AAA Louisville. Jordan could have put together a solid career as a football player, but the Cardinals offered him thrice his NFL salary to play baseball exclusively, and Jordan must have taken it as a challenge.

Eventually he'd star on the 1996 Cardinals squad that just missed the World Series, but before that Brian Jordan had already earned himself an unbreakable record of his very own: His five interceptions are the most in St. Louis Baseball Cardinals history.

Redbird Reference

Ozzie Smith

From the moment he showed up on Busch Stadium's sweltering Astroturf, Ozzie Smith was as brilliant as anticipated on defense, but few could have predicted he'd end up such a great hitter, too. That was how Ozzie Smith worked—he set expectations high and exceeded them anyway.

It's easy to forget, in hindsight, just how controversial Ozzie Smith's arrival in St. Louis was. Garry Templeton, the shortstop the Cardinals traded straight-up for Smith, had only five seasons earlier made one of the most impressive debuts in history, hitting .322 with 200 hits and 18 triples at just 21 years old. At the time, with shortstops hitting worse than ever as a group, that was difficult to overvalue.

But the team was changing rapidly under new manager Whitey Herzog, and when Templeton got into it that August with some Busch Stadium fans and made an obscene gesture, his ticket out of town had been punched. Smith, locked in a contract dispute in San Diego, made the perfect challenge trade: silver-slugging hitter for gold gloved fielder.

Unfortunately for the Padres, the Cardinals ended up with Smith, rail-thin at 5'11", who was rarely a threat for extra bases. But in St. Louis he turned into a remarkably pesky hitter, slapping singles and drawing walks so effectively that he eventually won an improbable Silver Slugger-Gold Glove combo in 1987. That ability to get on base, combined with his speed, made him one of the best-hitting shortstops of his light-hitting era. The player who got the bat knocked out of his hands in 1981, when he slugged just .256, finished his career with an above-average on-base percentage.

But his defense was always the main attraction. On the Astroturfed fields of the 1980s, which gave high and predictable bounces, Smith's defense looked not just wizardly but clairvoyant—he could chase down a baseball's bounces in advance, and later on when arm injuries robbed him of strength and accuracy, he began throwing remarkably precise on a carefully timed hop.

It was natural talent that made him brilliant, but it was that incredible baseball sense, that infield intuition, that kept him brilliant a decade after most shortstops had been moved off the position and then retired. As he slowed, as his arm faltered, even as he struggled to stay on the field, Smith played outstanding defense. He was simply better than everyone else at everything it takes to be a shortstop, and he was for nearly 20 years.

That combination of time and brilliance made Ozzie Smith a St. Louis institution, although the backflips on his way out to the infield didn't hurt. Arriving at Busch Stadium after a long dry spell, personifying the team's first World Championship in 15 years, Smith was the only constant presence through three pennants in the 1980s and another dry spell in the 1990s. By his retirement in 1996, he'd seen one generation of Cardinals and the dawn of the next with Tony La Russa's appearance.

By then Smith had become inimitably popular, not just around St. Louis but across baseball. At 41 years old he'd earned 15 All-Star berths and 13 Gold Gloves, and his victory lap of the National League was one of the great stories of the season.

Smith was the perfect player for a victory lap; nobody could see him do what he did—barehand grounders at shortstop, backflip, or just grin like he'd never stopped playing baseball for fun—and dislike him.

coming near this mark. Since Musial's career ended only Lou Brock has topped 100 triples with the Cardinals, finishing at 121. After that there's just Willie McGee with 83.

5. Lou Brock's 888 stolen bases. The flip-side of McGwire's 70 home runs, Brock's stolen bases came in a historical moment that was uniquely suited for relentless, reckless base-stealing. It was before the home run made stolen bases a dangerous proposition; before purist baseball fans made Astroturf an anathema; before sabermetrics calculated the exact break-even point for bag-thievery.

And it came from a player who arrived fully formed at that exact moment and kept outrunning the baseball until he was 40 years old. Unless the next Busch Stadium's center field wall is 500' from

home plate, we're unlikely to see a challenger to Brock's career or single-season records any time soon.

6. Bob Gibson's 1.12 ERA. Gibby's 1968 would be one of the greatest pitching seasons of all time no matter where it had occurred—in Coors Field circa 2000, at the height of the dead ball era, in Silver King's pitching box— but that impossible number 1.12, half again as low as his next-lowest ERA, came in the canonical Year of the Pitcher, the season everyone stopped scoring runs at once.

That year the Cardinals' top slugging percentage belonged to Lou Brock, who scraped out a .418 mark thanks to his 14 triples. Their top run producer was Mike Shannon, who drove in 79, and their top scorer was Brock, who needed every part of those 14 triples, 46 doubles, and 62 stolen bases to score 92 runs. And that was the fourth best offense in the National League! Meanwhile, the New York Mets and Los Angeles Dodgers each managed a lower team OPS (on-base plus slugging percentage) than light-hitting Mike Matheny did in his career.

It was a different kind of baseball, and the year it happened

Bob Gibson was the most dominant pitcher on planet Earth. The only way anyone will ever approach it again is if every hitter in Major League Baseball simultaneously forgets Babe Ruth existed, and begins slapping the ball to the infielders and trying to run out ground balls.

John Tudor is the only other starter since World War II to

Redbird Reference
Austin McHenry

In 1921, three seasons into his major league career, an unnamed baseball executive told a magazine that Austin McHenry was the best left fielder he'd ever seen. McHenry had just finished hitting .350 with 37 doubles, 17 home runs, and 13 outfield assists from his cannon of an arm. He was 25 years old.

In August of 1922 he was out of baseball, and in November he was dead.

That's the sad, incredible story of Austin McHenry, a Cardinals great that could have been but wasn't. As late as June 1922, everything seemed to be all right with the Cardinals' young slugger, but Branch Rickey, who'd scouted McHenry and would go to his grave disclaiming about his brilliance, noticed something was amiss when McHenry—known already for how easy everything he did appeared to look—struggled to track down routine fly balls.

McHenry told Rickey he'd been having trouble seeing and was sent home to Ohio to rest. A month later he returned, but only for a series—Rickey could tell he wasn't well and sent him back again.

In the fall McHenry was finally sent to a hospital, where they discovered he had a brain tumor. An operation in October failed, although recovery seemed like a possibility. But by November things had gotten worse and he was sent home to die.

He'd hit .303 that year, just well enough that his career line will confuse every new generation of baseball fans who stumble across his entry in the encyclopedia. And any of them who look further will only find more questions, and a small set of sad facts, waiting for them.

appear on the Cardinals' top-ten single-season ERA list courtesy of his brilliant season in 1985.

That's just one of the records Bob Gibson isn't likely to relinquish any time soon. His complete games and shutouts are untouchable in the seven-reliever era, and with 250 innings tougher to reach every season, his 3,884.1 would require a starter to lead the league about 15 seasons running. And while he's at it, his 24 home runs as a pitcher lead Cardinals starters by just as wide a margin.

7. Jesse Burkett's 185 singles. If you want to know what players like Jesse Burkett, turn of the century star of the St. Louis Perfectos and Browns, looked like, imagine Ichiro. Burkett's 185 singles in 1899 are the 12th most any player has ever managed in a single season, and the only players on the same list are "Wee" Willie Keeler, Lloyd Waner, and Ichiro, 100 years removed from all those nineteenth-century stars.

Ichiro aside, unless the Cardinals sign their own slap-hitting savant, the days of 185 singles in 221 base hits are probably over.

8. Albert Pujols' Intentional Walks. Pujols has all those unbreakable and nigh-unbreakable Stan Musial records to deal with, but there's one place in which he's already made his mark—intentional walks.

A relatively recent introduction into the baseball record books,

Pujols averaged 24 intentional walks a year in his first 10 seasons as National League pitchers found themselves increasingly terrified of the Cardinals' first baseman, peaking at 44.

But with sabermetric thought increasingly turned against the intentional walk as a strategy, Pujols may be the last of the Cardinals' stars to get avoided quite so frequently. It's impossible to tell yet whether the intentional walk is tomorrow's stolen base, but that's how records work.

Records are made to be broken because the moment you can't reach them they become impossible to fathom—they cease to become records at all, at least of anything you can imagine.

Short of stepping into a time machine, dressing yourself in an exceedingly baggy, heavy uniform with a tiny wool cap, and swinging an impossibly heavy bat against Silver King yourself, it's impossible to know what winning 45 games in a season—pitching almost half your team's games—even looks like. Only a few years after the fact it's become difficult to consider anybody hitting 60 home runs in a season, let alone 70.

These records might be dormant or little more than relics of baseball's many different phases, but that's never once kept Cardinals fans from celebrating the weirdest and most outstanding.

Chapter 12

THE ST. LOUIS BROWNS' SAD HISTORY

It's strange considering their eventual anonymity, and ironic in a cruel way, like much of their history. The St. Louis Browns everyone knows began as a tribute to one of the greatest franchises of the 1880s. Those Browns, the eventual Cardinals, were trailblazers—the first team to consider the idea of the World Series and the model franchise of the American Association.

These Browns, the American League models, were perhaps the worst team in the history of baseball.

Somebody had to be. But as the Browns recede further from memory—as the idea of a team attempting to compete with the St. Louis Cardinals anywhere within the city limits becomes more absurd—it becomes more important to remember that sad history.

It's more important still to remember that the Browns began their time in Major League Baseball on nearly even footing with the National League club that would eventually be the Cardinals. In 1902, when they moved from Milwaukee to become the Browns in just the second year of the rebel American League's existence, they stole all-world shortstop Bobby Wallace from the Cardinals, making him the highest-paid player in baseball.

That year they finished second in the nascent league, 20 games over .500 thanks to strong seasons from Wallace and three-time batting champion Jesse Burkett, another turncoat from the Cardinals. Meanwhile those Cardinals had fallen from fourth in the National League to sixth. At that point, things could have gone anywhere. Were it not for an improbable World Series win, you could be holding in your hands at this very moment, *The Ultimate St. Louis Browns Record Book.*

For years the Browns routinely outdrew the Cardinals, with both teams struggling on the

Redbird Reference

Eddie Gaedel

It is only fitting that the St. Louis Browns' most famous player, after George Sisler, has become Eddie Gaedel, a 3'7" publicity stunt cooked up in the most overheated section of Bill Veeck's publicity-stunted brain. In 1951 Gaedel donned the 1/8 jersey—not quite retired but never used again—and drew a four-pitch walk.

Veeck-as-in-wreck, who'd purchased the basement-dwelling Browns after selling the Cleveland Indians to settle his divorce, had more stunts planned for after Gaedel—later there was Grandstand Manager's Day, in which fans voted on in-game strategy and broke a four-game losing streak—but nothing quite matched the sight of Sportsman's Park personnel wheeling a 7' birthday cake out onto the field with the newest Brown inside during the bottom of the first inning.

Wearing the jersey of future Cardinals owner (and present 9-year-old) Bill DeWitt, Gaedel came out to raucous cheers as a pinch-hitter for leadoff man Frank Saucier. Bob Cain, the Detroit Tigers' starter and Veeck's unwitting accomplice, was finally cajoled into pitching—after four balls missed Gaedel's minute strike zone, the Browns had their leadoff hitter on base.

A day later, the American League's mystified president voided the contract, ending the career of the Browns' most dangerous hitter of the 1950s after one day. Three years later, they were the Baltimore Orioles.

Contemporary Comparo: There's no way to make this comparison without getting some unwitting utility infielder's contract voided by Bud Selig.

field. In 1920, with George Sisler the marquee name in St. Louis baseball, the Browns topped the Cardinals by nearly 75,000 paid fans with both teams under .500.

Things didn't change until 1926 when the Cardinals chased their first pennant and World Series championship while the Browns' attendance cratered by comparison. The Browns never recovered; they only barely competed.

The next two decades weren't kind to the Browns—all at once they'd become the second team

in a city that seemed suddenly unable or unwilling to support it. Sisler left, and nobody was there to replace him—the most famous Brown after Sisler was probably Eddie Gaedel, their 3'7" pinch hitter.

Even the St. Louis Browns' only American League pennant couldn't be uncomplicated by their status as perennial inter league, intracity doormats. It was 1944, with World War II decimating talent across baseball, when they finally found themselves atop the American

St. Louis Browns All-Time Hitting Leaders

Statistic	Player	Total	Years
Most Games Played	George Sisler	1,647	1915–27
Most Hits	George Sisler	2,295	1915–27
Most Doubles	George Sisler	343	1915–27
Most Triples	George Sisler	145	1915–27
Most Home Runs	Ken Williams	185	1918–27
Most Stolen Bases	George Sisler	351	1915–27
Most Runs Scored	George Sisler	1,091	1915–27
Most Runs Batted In	George Sisler	959	1915–27
Highest Batting Average	George Sisler	.344	1915–27
Highest On-Base Percentage	Ken Williams	.403	1918–27
Highest Slugging Percentage	Ken Williams	.558	1918–27
Highest On-Base Plus Slugging (OPS)	Ken Williams	.961	1918–27

St. Louis Browns All-Time Pitching Leaders

Statistic	Player	Total	Years
Most Games Pitched	Elam Vangilder	323	1919–27
Most Wins	Urban Shocker	126	1918–24
Most Losses	Jack Powell	143	1902–12
Most Innings Pitched	Jack Powell	2,229.2	1901–12
Most Shutouts	Jack Powell	27	1901–12
Most Strikeouts	Jack Powell	884	1901–12
Most Walks	Dixie Davis	640	1920–26
Best Earned Run Average	Harry Howell	2.06	1904–10

League after a long run of second-division mediocrity.

The team didn't look much like a pennant-winner, to say the least—composed of aging major leaguers and minor league stars, 4-Fs who couldn't be drafted, and players hadn't had their name called, they stunned the American League on their way to an 89–65 season with a set of players so diverse as to include, by 1945, the one-armed outfielder Pete Gray, who'd topped .300 in the minor leagues but was finally unable to time his swing for breaking pitches.

And if that weren't enough, the National League's champions that year were the most dominant team of World War II and the Browns' more illustrious roommates, Billy Southworth's three-time defending National League Champion St. Louis Cardinals.

There was one pleasant surprise for St. Louis fans who got together for the Streetcar Series—each team's 23-year-old superstar was still in the United States. The Cardinals still had Stan Musial,

a year removed from leading baseball in doubles, triples, hits, and batting average. The Browns, for their part, still had shortstop Vern "Buster" Stephens, who'd led the American League in RBIs and nearly led it in home runs.

But whatever offensive showdown the Sportsman's Park faithful might have hoped for, they were sorely disappointed—Musial was his usual self, hitting .304 with a home run, but Stephen's power was neutralized by the Cardinals' ace pitchers. Mort Cooper and Max Lanier each started twice, with Lanier closing out the series in six.

That was the end of the Browns, for the most part—but in perfect Browns fashion there was more whimpering to do. Ten years of second-division finishes later, including five consecutive last or second-to-last-place seasons, and the Browns were the Baltimore Orioles, leaving the Cardinals alone in St. Louis for the first time since 1902.

The St. Louis Browns All-Time Lineup

In general, Browns either weren't good enough to go elsewhere or weren't eager to stick around. But with some small effort we have successfully devised the following All-Time Browns Lineup.

Catcher: Rick Ferrell (1929–33, 1941–43) or Hank Severeid (1915–25)

Hank Severeid, who caught for the Browns between 1915 and 1925, is clearly the best in Browns history, but how can you pass up a real, live Hall of Famer like Rick Ferrell, who might be the worst real, live Hall of Famer there is? (And who caught for the Browns from 1929–33 and 1941–43?)

Severeid could get on base and had a very good arm. He's the kind of catcher you can win a championship with, which is probably not what the All-Time Browns were hoping to shoot for. It's the ultimate Browns decision—do you want the best player, or the one who was just good enough to stick around?

First Base: George Sisler (1915–27)

George Sisler is the St. Louis Browns. He's the one who held records, the one who was considered among the best of the best, the only one who earned himself a statue outside the second Busch Stadium in a row that the Browns have never played in.

For a certain generation of statistical experts, he was also a bit of a punching bag—the singles-hitter who was overrated after returning from a debilitating case of sinusitis in 1923.

But before that sinusitis cost him a full season of baseball and his power, Sisler was an incomparable talent—a kind of Super Ichiro, who at the dawn of the live ball era managed to dominate a slugger's position with a combination of unmatched contact-hitting, defense, and baserunning skills. His two .400 seasons are anything but empty—in 1920 he hit 49 doubles, 18 triples, and 19 home runs to go into his 257 hits, and in 1922 he hit 18 more triples and stole 51 bases while hitting .420.

The sinusitis changed him forever and prematurely shortened a career that could have gone on another 10 years. But that's no reason to forget the remarkable career he did have.

Second Base: Del Pratt (1912–17)

We are unable to confirm at this date that Del Pratt is a real person, but he had an excellent rookie season with the Browns in 1912, hitting .300 with walks and power and putting together four more solid years, winning an RBI crown in 1916 before being traded to the New York Yankees for, among other things, the great and great-named Urban Shocker.

Pratt was a member of the Yankees in time for the start of Babe Ruth's home run binge before ending up with the Red Sox.

Third Base: Harlond Clift (1934–43)

On a borderline Hall of Fame path before he fell off, the Browns' decision to trade their power-hitting star third baseman in the middle of his first down year is perhaps the luckiest they ever got. Over nine seasons with the Browns, the 30-year-old had hit .280 and averaged 19 home runs and 83 RBIs a year. When he was sent to the Washington Senators in 1943, he hit just .212 in three more seasons before retiring.

The Browns' intuition was even more impressive at the time, because Clift's career was more impressive. When he hit 29 home runs in 1937, he set the all-time record for home runs by a third baseman. He was a transitional player, one of the first third basemen who was more likely to hit for power than chase down bunts and slap singles.

And for once, the Browns got things exactly right—it was just a Browns-sized shame that it involved one of their very best players coming to a rapid and premature end as a difference-maker.

Shortstop: Bobby Wallace (1902–16)

This is one of the most distinctly unfair facts of St. Louis baseball. Bobby Wallace, the best shortstop in Browns history, had his best year as a Cardinal. Wallace, one of the best defensive players of his generation, put up an outstanding season for the Cardinals in 1901 and jumped a year later to the upstart American League and its Browns, becoming the best-paid player in baseball.

He was great for the Browns, too, but not quite that great. After their brilliant bursting onto the American League scene in 1902, Wallace and the Browns were never quite that good again, floating around the second division until Wallace, at 43 years old, returned to the Cardinals as a bit player in 1917.

Left Field: George Stone (1905–10)

The Browns have one significant advantage over the All-Time Cardinals, and it's this: much better names. And we haven't even gotten to Baby Doll Jacobson yet. George Stone is the perfect name for their best-ever left fielder, whose nickname was Silent George and who came out of nowhere to have a peak Albert Pujols season at 29. Who was born, seriously, in some place called Lost Nation,

Iowa, and he disappeared just as abruptly as he'd appeared in 1910, having put together four outstanding seasons and two average ones.

Stone was a minor league slugger and apparently an accomplished violinist, but he cuts a somewhat more mysterious figure on the baseball card—after his stint as the American League's top hitter, he apparently decided on the violin.

Center Field: Baby Doll Jacobson (1915–26)
Now we've gotten to Baby Doll Jacobson! Born in a coal-mining town to people who probably didn't think Baby Doll was as great a name as history does, Jacobson, another late bloomer, hit .350 two years in a row after earning a full-time job with the Browns.

He was like a poor baby-doll's Jim Edmonds—arriving at a full-time job with the Browns, baseball's halfway house, in his late 20s, Jacobson managed to stick around as an excellent defensive center fielder until he was 35.

Right Field: Ken Williams (1918–27)
The strangest of all the Browns' strange late-bloomers, Ken Williams exists primarily as an unintentionally mysterious enigma in the baseball record books. Why'd he start so late? Why'd he bounce around so long in the minor leagues, and how was he so good once he'd arrived?

One of the first players after Babe Ruth to discover fire and the home run ball, Williams topped the Babe himself in 1922 to lead the AL with 39 home runs and 155 RBIs, not to mention 37 stolen bases—nobody was particularly impressed at the time, but it was baseball's first 30/30 season.

These All-Time Browns aren't quite the Cardinals, stocked with Hall of Famers at every position, but they represent the Browns as they existed and before they were little more than a beaten-down caricature—mixed with all the disappointments were some truly strange and striking moments, from that 1944 pennant run to Bill Veeck's antics to George Sisler's brilliant hitting.

Chapter 13

St. Louis and Chicago Play the Lost World Series in 1885
World Series Facts

Chris Von der Ahe, owner of the American Association St. Louis Browns that would later become the National League Cardinals, was an innovator, and luckily for baseball most of his innovations never stuck. The man who called himself "Der Poss Bresident" in his comically thick accent was a trailblazer for bad baseball ideas; nearly every terrible decision an owner can make today was made by Von der Ahe in the 1880s.

1. He inserted himself into the conversation—despite knowing little about baseball, he named himself manager three separate times, once assured his press agent that the "American people" would rather hear about him than "read about them ballplayers," and finally constructed a statue of himself outside Sportsman's Park, which one wag titled, "Von der Ahe Discovers Illinois."

2. He overspent and eventually paid for it—between his lavish spending and the women euphemistically referred to in the press (and eventually used as a nickname for the Browns) as "Coochie Coochies," Von der Ahe successfully bankrupted himself and nearly bankrupted the Cardinals, forcing him to sell off the team's best players and leading to a 10-year swoon after the team moved from the Association to the National League.

3. He created the first mall park—a hundred years before fans worried about today's baseball stadiums filling up with distractions, Von der Ahe constructed his crowning achievement, a ball field surrounded by an amusement park, a beer garden, race tracks in the outfield, a log flume, and an artificial lake. The ballpark earned the name "Coney Island West" from press who had also dubbed the owner Von der Ha Ha.

For all that, though, Von der Ahe also introduced some innovations that remain in baseball even today. Thirty years before Branch Rickey had the idea, Von der Ahe created a rudimentary farm team to feed his Browns players, although it took him only a month to grow tired of the concept and attempt to sell his St. Louis Whites. And anyone who considers beer and a brat fundamental to his enjoyment

of a baseball game should pour one out for Von der Ahe, who purchased his team only after realizing what he could make on concessions.

But the most vital of his fantasies—which, like most everything he did, he failed to follow through to its logical conclusion—was none other than the spectacle of the World Series.

When he challenged the National League champions to a 12-game barnstorming series after the 1885 regular season, he wasn't just arranging a national baseball championship—he was also, inadvertently, beginning another St. Louis tradition, the cutthroat rivalry with the Chicago Cubs.

They were the White Stockings then—as happened in St. Louis, an American League team was eventually named after them—and they were baseball royalty, owned by Al Spalding and managed by Cap Anson, two of the most important figures at the dawn of professional baseball in 1871. In the unbalanced National League they'd gone an incredible 87–25, two games ahead of the New York Giants and 32 games ahead of any other team.

With Anson still a dangerous hitter and King Kelly, the most famous man in baseball, patrolling the outfield, they were the class of baseball's first two decades, and in hindsight they really had nothing to gain by accepting Von der Ahe's offer.

The Browns—79–33 in their own right—had everything to gain. The American Association was just four years old and it was still regarded skeptically by the baseball establishment that saw it as an outlaw league promoted in cities with no moral fiber to fans who could afford its cheaper tickets. The teetotaler National League clubs and their supporters eventually derided it as the "Beer and Whiskey League," because alcohol sales were legal at its parks.

The Browns, a hard-charging group who played to crowds plied with Von der Ahe's libations, represented the best and most notorious aspects of American Association play. Comiskey was respected throughout baseball, but with players like the practical joker Arlie Latham on the field and Von der Ahe in the owners' box, they were hardly the model of a staid, respectable National League club.

Of course, the World Series wasn't the very model of a staid, respectable National League institution. Held in four ballparks, three of them Association-affiliated (and thus able to sell the eponymous beer and whiskey), the series was half a competition and half a money-making tour staked to $1,000 by the teams' owners.

Game 1 ended in a 5–5 tie on account of darkness, and that was the most conventional game of the series. In Game 2 Comiskey pulled the Browns from the field in protest of the umpire's work with the White Stockings leading 5–4 in the sixth inning. The *Globe-Democrat* reported after the game of an altercation between the Vice President of the Browns and Cap Anson, described in 19th Century newswriting style as "the Friend of the Laboring Man" versus Anson's "Big Captain of the Chicago Team."

Squabbles over the rules—American Association or National League?—the comportment of the players—the White Stockings' King Kelly was as guilty as any Brown—and the success of the series—just 500 people saw Game 5, played deep into a cold October in neutral Pittsburgh—dogged the series all the way up to Game 7, when the Browns defeated Chicago 13–4 behind Dave Foutz.

Which is where it got messier still. The Browns claimed Game 2 didn't count; the White Stockings declared it a forfeit. After some wrangling the teams agreed to split the $1,000 prize, with Spalding and Von der Ahe's money never changing hands.

In the 1880s, a series could simultaneously be an unruly amalgam of fights and called games and a major success. In 1886 the Browns won 93 games, the White Stockings won 90 more, and Comiskey's Browns this time left no room for doubt—they won in six games thanks to strong hitting from Tip O'Neill and a pitching staff that solved both Anson and Kelly. The Browns were finally the best baseball team in the world, and the American Association had finally, if briefly, established itself as the equal of the Senior Circuit.

The Browns were a dynasty, and in any other hands that might have been good news. But it went, inevitably, to Von der Ahe's head. When the Detroit Wolverines won the National League pennant, their owner, Frederick Stearns, and Von der Ahe set out to make the 1887 World Series into the biggest spectacle in the history of baseball.

Von der Ahe knew spectacle. The men planned a 15-game extravaganza—this series would begin in St. Louis and Detroit and end touring the East Coast, each fan paying an extraordinary $1 for the privilege of general admission. It spanned nearly the entire month of October, even accounting for a morning-afternoon doubleheader that took place in Washington D.C. and Baltimore.

It was all in keeping with Von der Ahe's tastes. The 1887 Series, a gaudy Super Bowl for a time before national TV, was perhaps the absolute zenith of his strange legacy. But the Browns, the much stronger team, were beaten up and down the eastern seaboard. They were beaten in St. Louis when Dave Foutz couldn't keep runs off the board early; they were beaten in Detroit when Bob Caruthers

the hitter was the only Browns batter who could hit behind Bob Caruthers the pitcher. They were beaten in Baltimore and Brooklyn and most everywhere else.

The bats were silenced. Even Tip O'Neill, who hit what was called .492 at the time and had one of the best seasons in baseball history, couldn't make a dent in the Wolverines' no-name pitching staff. (The immortal Charles "Lady" Baldwin and Pretzels Getzien won eight games in 11 chances.)

To make matters more unpleasant—for the players and fans, at least—the Browns had to play the series out after the Wolverines had clinched, with Detroit celebrating all the while. The last game was called because of cold and darkness just three days before the series spilled into November.

The $6,000 Von der Ahe made on the loss—Stearns pocketed $18,000, or $400,000 adjusted for inflation—did little to placate Der Mercurial Poss Bresident. The man whose statue stood in front of the ballpark told the *Globe-Democrat* that he'd hoped his team had gotten the "big head" knocked out of it.

What that meant, apparently, was that he'd knock the big head right out of it. Von der Ahe seized on his team's attitude as the reason for their failings, and he seized on the reason for their attitude as nobody but his star player, Bob Caruthers himself. "Parisian Bob," as he became known after a trans-Atlantic contract dispute, was a one-of-a-kind player, at one point the best hitter and the best pitcher in the league, but he was also an inveterate gambler and man-about-town. He and the other Browns had probably enjoyed their tour of the east coast's major cities for reasons that did not stop at ballpark variety.

Never mind Von der Ahe's *own* propensity for gambling and manning about town—Caruthers' telegraphic negotiations had endeared himself less to his owner than they had to the press, and he was soon sold, with some of his partners in crime, to the Brooklyn Bridegrooms.

The Browns would never be the same. Von der Ahe was rarely flush even when times were good, and as the team drifted down the league standings and his other business ventures went bust, they became the laughing stock of baseball. By the time they were finally sold to the Robisons in 1898, the Browns, who had so dominated the American Association, had finished 11th or 12th in the league in six of their seven National League seasons.

The name was so damaged that few tears were shed when the Robisons decided to change the name—first to the Perfectos, and then, after an off-handed comment about their new uniforms, the Cardinals.

1926 World Series

After a long, painful gestation—the American League Browns routinely outdrew their National League counterpart in their early years together—the modern Cardinals finally emerged in 1926, winning the World Series and separating themselves permanently from their hapless roommates.

Armed with Rogers Hornsby, the best hitter in the National League, and Bob O'Farrell, the forgotten 1926 NL MVP, keying the league's best offense, the 1926 squad is most famous now for their washed-up swingman, Grover Cleveland "Pete" Alexander, and his gutty performance in Games 6 and 7.

After his complete-game win in Game 6, Alexander—an alcoholic who some thought was drunk or at least hung over at the time—was called upon in the seventh inning of Game 7 with the bases loaded, two away, and the Cardinals staked to a 3–2 lead. With no margin for error, he struck out Yankees star Tony Lazzeri and held on through two more innings to clinch the Cardinals' first modern World Series.

Game 7 famously ended with a play that rings totally dissonant to modern ears—Babe Ruth, with two outs and the winning run at the plate, was thrown out attempting to steal second base. Apparently people forgot about Bob O'Farrell even then.

1928 WORLD SERIES

The revenge of Babe Ruth—Ruth goes 10–16 with three home runs. Pete Alexander has an ERA of 19.80, and the Cardinals are swept in four games. No word as to the condition of little Johnny Sylvester.

1930 WORLD SERIES

The Cardinals' incredible bats— they'd scored 1,004 runs in the regular season—fall silent all at once against the Philadelphia Athletics, who top them in six games for their fifth World Series championship.

In Game 4 Jesse Haines manages to outduel the great Lefty Grove only for Grove to come back in Game 5 and earn a win in relief on zero days' rest.

1931 WORLD SERIES

An improved Cardinals team upsets an even more-improved 107-win Athletics club in seven games for their second World Series title. Pepper Martin, "The Wild Horse of the Osage" and the only new contributor to the Cardinals' stacked order, goes 12–24 with four doubles and a home run.

Burleigh Grimes, one of the last pitchers legally allowed to throw the spitball, outpitches Grove in Game 3 and wins Game 7 handily

Remember When...

Any story you've ever heard about a star player hitting a home run for a sick child begins with the 1926 World Series when the baseball-crazy press caught wind of a story that Babe Ruth had promised to hit a home run for a critically ill 11-year-old just before whacking three of them in Game 4.

Little Johnny Sylvester, the newspapers reported in turn, made a miraculous and complete recovery, living to the ripe old age of 74.

in the last full season of his 19-year major league career.

1934 WORLD SERIES

The Gashouse Gang wins another nailbiter thanks to the brothers Dean—Dizzy won Games 1 and 7, while Paul took care of Games 3 and 6. Of course, Dizzy also lost Game 5 and broke up a double play attempt as a pinch runner in Game 4 by putting his head between the baseball and the Detroit Tigers' first baseman.

X-Rays, as they say, revealed nothing.

1942 WORLD SERIES

Stan Musial hits just .222 but the 106-win Cardinals top the Yankees anyway in six games. Little Johnny

Sylvester is 27 years old and still healthy even though Babe Ruth retired in 1935.

1943 World Series
The Yankees get the better of a much better Cardinals team despite losing Joe DiMaggio to the war effort.

1944 World Series
The Cardinals grab both of the St. Louis Browns' hands and begin slapping the Browns' face with them while saying, "Why are you hitting yourself? Why are you hitting yourself?"

The Browns' only AL pennant saw them lose in six games to the team that shared their ballpark. It's tough being the little brother.

1946 World Series
Enos Slaughter is back in uniform after spending four years in a different uniform and makes the most of it on his famous Mad Dash—standing on first base with two outs in the eighth inning of Game 7, the score tied at three, Slaughter was off with the pitch and, when outfielder Harry Walker lofted a base hit into left field, blew through the third base coach's stop sign despite the ball having already reached the relay man at shortstop.

Slaughter reached home just ahead of the bewildered shortstop's throw and scored the run, which held up as the series winner. The Boston Red Sox weren't quite

cursed yet, but in hindsight this one was lumped in with the rest of the Bambino's nefarious schemes.

1964 World Series
The Cardinals win their seventh World Series championship, and their third against the Yankees, in seven games thanks to an incredible performance from Bob Gibson, who won Game 7 on two days' rest.

1967 World Series
Bob Gibson, still recovering from the effects of a broken leg, carries the Cardinals again, winning Games 1, 5, and 7 for El Birdos. Lou Brock scores eight runs and drives in three more, while newly acquired Roger Maris drives in seven himself.

1968 World Series
Even Bob Gibson can't win them all—despite outdueling 30-game-winner Denny McLain in Games 1 and 4 and hitting a home run, he loses a decisive Game 7 against Mickey Lolich, dropping his career World Series record all the way to 7–2 with an ERA of 1.89.

Lou Brock hits .464 in the Year of the Pitcher.

1982 World Series
Whitey Herzog's makeover of the disappointing teams of the 1970s pays off—armed with a new shortstop (Ozzie Smith), a new closer (Bruce Sutter), and

a rookie named Willie McGee, the fleet-footed Cardinals top the slugging Milwaukee Brewers in seven games.

1985 WORLD SERIES

The I-70 Series pits the best of the Whiteyball Cardinals teams against a solid Royals squad and both teams against the specter of bad umpiring when first base umpire Don Denkinger misses a clear call at first base and the Cardinals implode in Games 6 and 7.

1987 WORLD SERIES

The last of the Whiteyball pennant winners is unable to take a single game at the Metrodome as the underdog Minnesota Twins beat the Cardinals in seven games.

A generation of Cardinals fans laments the thought of an 85–77 team winning the World Series (until 2006) and looks skeptically at air conditioners after hearing rumors that the currents in the Metrodome were being manipulated to benefit Kent Hrbek.

2004 WORLD SERIES

After nine years, Tony La Russa gets the Cardinals into the World Series with one of the best teams in club history—the MV3 Cardinals, led by Albert Pujols, Jim Edmonds, and Scott Rolen, who rolled into the World Series with 105 wins.

Unfortunately, all those years of perpetuating the Curse of the

Behind the Numbers

World Series games prior to 1903, when the American League and the National League began playing the first official championship series in Major League Baseball, are considered exhibitions in the official record.

Bambino turn catastrophic when the Red Sox sweep the Cardinals in four games and film the ending to *Fever Pitch*, a Jimmy Fallon movie about being an obnoxious Red Sox fan, on the field at Busch Stadium.

2006 WORLD SERIES

The MV3 Cardinals, dogged at every turn by injuries, limp into the postseason, defeat the New York Mets in one of the most tense NLCS matchups of all time, and beat the Detroit Tigers in five games as penance for 2004.

Nobody expects to see anything like it again

2011 WORLD SERIES

People see something like it again as the Cardinals win their 11th World Series championship. Three different managers pitch to David Freese several times and regret it when he sweeps the postseason MVP trophies and saves the day multiple times in Games 6 and 7 of the World Series against the Texas Rangers.

Cardinals World Series Results

1885 World Series
St. Louis Browns tie Chicago White Stockings, 3 games to 3 (one tie, one forfeit)

1886 World Series
St. Louis Browns defeat Chicago White Stockings, 4 games to 2

1887 World Series
Detroit Wolverines defeat St. Louis Browns, 10 games to 5

1888 World Series
New York Giants defeat St. Louis Browns 6 games to 4

1926 World Series
St. Louis Cardinals defeat New York Yankees, 4 games to 3

1928 World Series
New York Yankees defeat St. Louis Cardinals, 4 games to 0

1930 World Series
Philadelphia Athletics defeat St. Louis Cardinals, 4 games to 2

1931 World Series
St. Louis Cardinals defeat Philadelphia Athletics, 4 games to 3

1934 World Series
St. Louis Cardinals defeat Detroit Tigers, 4 games to 3

1942 World Series
St. Louis Cardinals defeat New York Yankees, 4 games to 1

1943 World Series
New York Yankees defeat St. Louis Cardinals, 4 games to 1

1944 World Series
St. Louis Cardinals defeat St. Louis Browns, 4 games to 2

1946 World Series
St. Louis Cardinals defeat Boston Red Sox, 4 games to 3

1964 World Series
St. Louis Cardinals defeat New York Yankees, 4 games to 3

1967 World Series
St. Louis Cardinals defeat Boston Red Sox, 4 games to 3

1968 World Series
Detroit Tigers defeat St. Louis Cardinals, 4 games to 3

1982 World Series
St. Louis Cardinals defeat Milwaukee Brewers, 4 games to 3

1985 World Series
Kansas City Royals defeat St. Louis Cardinals, 4 games to 3

1987 World Series
Minnesota Twins defeat St. Louis Cardinals, 4 games to 3

2004 World Series
Boston Red Sox defeat St. Louis Cardinals, 4 games to 0

2006 World Series
St. Louis Cardinals defeat Detroit Tigers, 4 games to 1

2011 World Series
St. Louis Cardinals defeat Texas Rangers, 4 games to 3

CHAPTER 14

THE ROBISONS BUILD THE ST. LOUIS PERFECTOS

Single-Season Team Records

In 1898, the Chris Von der Ahe era of baseball in St. Louis came to a sad and abrupt end. A fire in his showpiece stadium, the much-derided "Coney Island of the West," pushed the Browns' overstretched owner into bankruptcy, and the struggling team was auctioned off to the highest bidders—who happened, strangely enough, to already own a baseball team, the Cleveland Spiders.

Frank and Stanley Robison, Ohio-area businessmen, had founded the Spiders in 1887 while Von der Ahe's Browns were still dominating the old American Association. Moving their franchise to the National League before the Association's collapse, the Robisons had turned their Spiders into a perennial first-division contender, but nothing had come of it—in 1898 they'd finished with 81 wins and just 70,000 paid customers, fifth and last in the National League, respectively. The disastrous Browns had neatly reversed that finish—they'd won just 39 games, last in baseball, but more than 150,000 fans ticked Von der Ahe's turnstiles.

The Robisons quickly saw an opportunity. Buying up the distressed Browns, they kept what passed for major league talent on that roster and, all at once, transferred every single Spider of merit to the St. Louis club, including the incomparable Cy Young, who'd already won 241 games with Cleveland.

It was a never-seen-again bounty of talent—Hall of Fame shortstop Bobby Wallace, Hall of Fame outfielder Jesse "Crab" Burkett, Hall of Very Good types like Cupid Childs, and for good measure, the Spiders' longtime player-manager, Patsy Tebeau.

It was a shrewd business move, and it saved baseball in St. Louis. The cruel part was that they forced the husk of the Cleveland Spiders back out for the 1899 season, stocked with a mix of has-beens and minor league washouts that was, without question, the worst team in the history of Major League Baseball.

Stanley Robison, who resented Cleveland's poor drawing power, was apparently seeking to punish his erstwhile fanbase—he ran the team as a "sideshow," and it showed. The Spiders drew 6,000 fans—total—before teams refused to travel to their home park and they began an endless road trip. Sportswriters called them the Wanderers; a local sportswriter elucidated the following comforts for watching a historically awful team:

- There is everything to hope for and nothing to fear.
- Defeats do not disturb one's sleep.
- An occasional victory is a surprise and a delight.
- There is no danger of any club passing you.

- You are not asked 50 times a day, "What was the score?" People take it for granted that you lost.

Things were not quite the same in St. Louis, where the Perfectos had the steep expectations of a St. Louis fanbase that hadn't seen winners since 1891 and a pair of businessmen who'd just torpedoed their hometown nine for a chance at higher attendance. The Perfectos were as popular as the Robisons had hoped—attendance

The Strange Story of the St. Louis Maroons

Fifteen years before the Perfectos, St. Louis was host to another attempt to stack the deck in favor of the home team when local millionaire Henry Lucas, looking to create a third major league, made the fatal mistake of loving his own club too much. That's the story of the aptly named St. Louis Maroons, who went 94–19 in their first season, 36–72 in their second, and were out of baseball just after their third.

Lucas, who was 25 when he decided he might like a baseball league of his own, managed to gin up enough investors to put franchises in some major cities—Milwaukee, Cincinnati, Boston, Chicago—and after that well ran dry, somewhat less major cities— Altoona and Wilmington. With that burst of enthusiasm, the Union Association was born.

Lucas had money to back his venture and interested parties to play and watch, but he also had the temperament of someone who plays baseball video games on the easiest setting—the best players pulled from the established National League and American Association seemed to end up, as if pulled by magnets, to the Maroons, who made a farce of the Association by getting out to an enormous pennant lead almost immediately.

Four franchises, underfunded and aware, presumably, that Lucas was treating the league like his own miniature railroad set, disbanded climbed to 374,000 that first season—but after a 19–6 start, they began treading water and falling back toward the second division.

It got so bad that in June they recalled veteran infielder Lave Cross, who'd been given the thankless job of managing the Cleveland Spiders, to St. Louis, where he plugged a hole at third base. The Spiders' offensive core, it turned out, had gotten old all at once—Tebeau and Childs struggled, and the pitching behind Young wasn't good enough to make up for it.

In the end the Perfectos finished in fifth place. The Robisons had gotten their wish— they'd put their franchise in a city where people would flock to watch a good team. What was left, then, was the creation of a good team.

There was also the matter of the name, which had proved a little inappropriate for the distinctly average club it denoted. The Robisons abandoned the brown stockings that had given

in midseason; the Milwaukee Brewers, historically placed second in the UA "pennant race," finished with a record of 8–4 after joining the league at the end of the season. They'd come in to replace Wilmington, who'd gone 2–16 and folded themselves after replacing the Philadelphia Keystones, who'd folded earlier in August.

The UA is listed, in the official MLB records, as a major league, but it's anybody's guess why. When Lucas pulled his Maroons out from the wreckage of the Association after the league folded, they went from first to worst, finishing with just 36 wins in the much stronger National League. Fred "Sure Shot" Dunlap, their star player, had put up astounding numbers in the UA, scoring 160 runs in 101 games, hitting 13 home runs, and batting .412. In the National League the next season, he hit a solid but distinctly less Ruthian .270 average with two home runs and 70 runs.

Lucas, for his part, had used up more of his inheritance than he'd anticipated in getting the Union Association off the ground and promptly putting it back there. By 1902, $40,000 in debt after some other unsuccessful sporting ventures, Lucas filed for bankruptcy, working later in life for the city of St. Louis.

Lucas wasn't entirely a ridiculous figure—he was a genuine patron of baseball when it was anything but an upper-class pursuit, and with the Union Association he fought to earn free-agency rights that players wouldn't actually have for another 90 years. But his inability to create balance in his nascent league proved that there is such a thing as too much success.

St. Louis baseball its name and identity for 25 years in favor of a more attractive red. As the story goes, a sportswriter heard a woman call it a "lovely shade of cardinal," and that was it—

the 1900 St. Louis Nationals were finally, permanently, the Cardinals.

The red birds would have to come later, but the name, luckily, had stuck.

100-Win Seasons

Year	Won	Lost	WP	Place	G	Manager
1931	101	53	.656	First	+13	Gabby Street
1942	106	48	.688	First	+2	Billy Southworth
1943	105	49	.682	First	+18	Billy Southworth
1944	105	49	.682	First	+14.5	Billy Southworth
1967	101	60	.627	First	+10.5	Red Schoendienst
1985	101	61	.623	First	+3	Whitey Herzog
2004	105	57	.648	First	+13	Tony La Russa
2005	100	62	.617	First	+11	Tony La Russa

Single-Season Team Records

Record	Number	Year or Date
Most Wins	106	1942
Fewest Wins	29	1897
Most Losses	111	1898
Fewest Losses	33	1883, 1885

Redbirds Reference

Ripper Collins

Most of the members of the Gashouse Gang have been permanently enshrined in Cardinals-fan memory thanks to the wild stunts they pulled on and off the field, but Ripper Collins, with his extremely evocative nickname, has faded into obscurity despite playing a major role in the 1934 Cardinals' 1,004-run season.

Ripper, with Frankie Frisch and Pepper Martin on the bases in front of him, drove in 128 runs while hitting .333 with 40 doubles and 12 triples.

Single-Season Team Batting Records

Record	Number	Year
Most Runs Scored	1,004	1934
Fewest Runs Scored	372	1908
Most Hits	1,732	1930
Fewest Hits	1,105	1908
Highest Batting Average	.314	1930
Lowest Batting Average	.223	1908
Most Singles	1,233	1920
Most Doubles	373	1939
Most Triples	96	1920
Most Home Runs	235	2000
Fewest Home Runs	10	1906
Most .300 Hitters	11	1930
Highest On-Base Plus Slugging	.843	1930
Lowest On-Base Plus Slugging	.554	1908
Most Stolen Bases	581	1887
Fewest Stolen Bases	17	1949

Single-Season Team Pitching Records

Record	Number	Year
Lowest ERA	2.09	1888
Highest ERA	6.17	1897
Most Complete Games	146	1904
Fewest Complete Games	2	2007, 2008
Most Shutouts	30	1968
Most Saves	57	2004
Fewest Hits Allowed	729	1882
Most Hits Allowed	1,610	1936
Fewest Home Runs Allowed	7	1882
Most Home Runs Allowed	210	2003
Fewest Runs Allowed	409	1883
Most Runs Allowed	1,088	1897
Fewest Bases on Balls	103	1882
Most Bases on Balls	701	1911
Most Strikeouts	1,130	1997
Fewest Strikeouts	207	1897

Single-Game Team Records

Record	Number	Opponent	Date
Most Runs Scored	28	Philadelphia	7/6/1929
Most Runs Allowed	28	Boston	9/3/1896
Most Hits	30	New York	6/1/1895
Most Home Runs	7	Brooklyn	5/7/1940
		Chicago	7/12/1996
Most Total Bases	49	Brooklyn	5/7/1940

CHAPTER 15

WHITEYBALL SETS THE PACE FOR THE 1980s
All-Star Records and Opening Day Starts

The St. Louis Cardinals have been blessed, among their many other gifts as 11-time World Series champions, with style. A great Cardinals team is rarely just great—they're great and zany, like the Gashouse Gang of the 1930s, or they're great and intense and eccentric, like Tony La Russa's 21st Century pennant-winners.

But no Cardinals team had a more consistent identity on the field than the "Whiteyball" teams managed by the eponymous White Rat himself, Whitey Herzog. Built for the Astroturf and far-off fences of Busch Stadium, clad in powder blue polyester, the Cardinals outplayed

the National League all through the 1980s on a combination of sterling defense, infuriating plate discipline, and most visibly, blazing speed.

It was a team that required a consistent vision—as a result, Whitey Herzog emerged as the omnipresent force behind the Cardinals, managing the team on the field and reorganizing it from the front office during a productive two-year stint as general manager.

By the time he was finished, a team that had run in place for most of a decade after Bob Gibson and Lou Brock retired was as strong as ever.

The team he'd inherited was filled with useful pieces that never quite seemed to congeal into a pennant contender, and when he arrived Herzog, who'd found similarly autocratic success in Kansas City, set about trading the pieces that didn't fit his style—no matter how useful or popular they were.

So star catcher Ted Simmons was traded—disastrously, as it turned out—for high-upside outfielder David Green and Dave LaPoint. Popular third baseman Ken Reitz was packaged with Leon Durham and shipped to the Cubs for closer Bruce Sutter, who would be deployed as early as the seventh inning if it suited Herzog. Most daringly, Herzog traded shortstop-of-the-future Garry Templeton straight up for another young shortstop, the Padres' Ozzie Smith, who had the defense-and-speed profile Herzog couldn't resist.

By 1982 the underachieving Cardinals had been remade entirely in Herzog's image, and it showed. From 117 stolen bases in 1980 they

Redbird Reference

Ted Simmons

Reaching the major leagues as an 18-year-old during the Cardinals' ill-fated 1968 run and finding himself traded to the Milwaukee Brewers just before the Cardinals would beat them in the 1982 World Series, Ted Simmons is the lost Cardinals superstar, the key figure in their National League interregnum. Underrated by anyone who didn't watch him play every day, Simmons is one of the best players ever to have the inexplicable misfortune of earning less than 5 percent of the vote on his first Hall of Fame ballot.

For those who tuned out during the Cardinals' spotty decade, here's what Ted Simmons did from his first full season at catcher—he hit like few other catchers ever have. A perennial .300 hitter with line drive power, Simmons earned six All-Star nods in 10 seasons as the Cardinals' Opening Day catcher and, when he was traded prior to the 1981 season, had slugged better than .500 four years running.

The offense-first switch-hitter wasn't Whitey Herzog's type, so Cardinals fans are left to wonder what might have been if he and the White Rat had gotten along—what might have been if Simmons would have had the chance to play on a Cardinals team as talented as he was. By the time he retired in 1988, after stints with the Brewers and Braves, Simmons had reached rarefied territory for a catcher—2,472 hits, 483 doubles, and 1,389 RBIs.

hit 200 in 1982, and everyone but catcher Darrell Porter and token slugger George Hendrick had at least 10. On defense they had all-time-great talents like Smith and Keith Hernandez propping up the lumbering Hendrick and the aptly nicknamed "Skates," left fielder Lonnie Smith.

The offensive makeover was easier to spot, but the attention the Cardinals' pitching staff received proved just as important. Sutter threw 102 innings out of the bullpen, leading baseball with 36 saves. And Joaquin Andujar, the self proclaimed One Tough Dominican Herzog had acquired in 1981, was slotted in above long-time Cardinal Bob Forsch to solidify the rotation. With a defense of that caliber (and expansive Busch Stadium) behind him, a pitcher like Forsch could afford to strike out just 2.7 batters per nine innings and still win 15 games.

After competing but ultimately coming up short in strike-complicated 1981, the Cardinals spent most of the 1982 season in a three-way dogfight in a balanced National League East. After June 4, when their first-half lead peaked at 5½ games, things tightened up—for a month, starting on June 19 and ending August 3, the Cardinals were never more than two games up or down in the standings.

Fifteen times that year they were tied for the division lead. It

Behind the Numbers

Stan Musial was in the Cardinals' Opening Day lineup 21 times across three different positions—10 times in left field, five times in right field and at first base, and once—1949—in center field.

wasn't until mid-September that the Phillies and the Expos finally fell back for good, thanks in part to a brilliant seven start run from Andujar, who went 5–0 with an ERA of 0.92 over the last month of the season.

That year the postseason played out as a virtual advertisement for Whiteyball. The Cardinals swept the Braves in three games to take the National League Championship Series and rolled into the club's first World Series since 1968 against their polar opposites—the Milwaukee Brewers, nicknamed "Harvey's Wallbangers" for their own particular offensive style.

That offense—which featured, fittingly enough, the exiled Ted Simmons at catcher—was everything Whitey Herzog had spent two years exterminating in St. Louis. Their 216 home runs were more than three times as many as the Cardinals hit. In the middle of their order, outfielders Ben Ogilvie and Gorman Thomas outhomered the Cardinals all by themselves.

The goal, for Harvey's Wallbangers, was to reach base and stay there until somebody let you walk home. Even their own Hall of Fame shortstop, Robin Yount, had hit 29 home runs that year—10 more than any Cardinal.

It was the ultimate battle of philosophies, and it began with an extended demonstration of every last tenet of wall-banging. In Game 1, in front of almost 54,000 fans at Busch Stadium, the Brewers put six runs on Bob Forsch and four more on the back of the bullpen. Yount and Paul Molitor, hitting atop the order, combined to go 9–12, while Ted Simmons homered. Even the Cardinals' defense faltered when Keith Hernandez's first-inning error led to two floodgate-opening unearned runs. Meanwhile, the Cardinals' ostensibly pesky offense managed just one walk and three hits against 17-game winner Mike Caldwell.

Midway through the third inning in Game 2, it looked for a moment like things were about to get out of hand. Against Cardinals starter John Stuper, the Brewers managed both to scrape together a run in the Whiteyball fashion—Molitor stole second, took third on a wild pitch, and scored on a groundout to make it 2–0—and put a run on the board more conventionally when Ted Simmons gave them a 3–0 lead

Behind the Numbers

The Cardinals have used the same Opening Day lineup twice in a row only once—in 1967 and 1968, when Tim McCarver, Orlando Cepeda, Julian Javier, Mike Shannon, Dal Maxvill, Lou Brock, Curt Flood, and Roger Maris backed up Bob Gibson.

with his second home run of the series.

In the bottom of the inning, the Cardinals finally got on the board against Don Sutton thanks to a rally led by Willie McGee, and in the sixth inning NLCS MVP Darrell Porter hit an RBI double to tie the game at 4.

In the late innings, the Cardinals held a crucial advantage. Their relief ace, Bruce Sutter, was healthy, while the Brewers' Rollie Fingers was out for the postseason. Herzog called for Sutter in the seventh inning, and he held down the Brewers long enough for the Brewers' diminished relief corps to walk in the game-winning run in the eighth inning.

Each game seemed to be a referendum on offensive styles. Game 3 saw the Cardinals top the Brewers in Milwaukee by a score of 6–2, thanks in part to defensive heroics undoing the Brewers' extra-base hits. McGee, who had shown incredible range in the outfield all season, made two beautiful plays to rob Brewers of extra bases, including scaling the wall in the ninth inning to keep Gorman Thomas inside County Stadium. (Of course, McGee also hit two home runs himself.)

In Game 4, the Brewers, innings away from falling behind 3–1 in the series, wiped away a 5–1 Cardinals lead when the bats came back on. Dave LaPoint's failure to pull in a feed from Hernandez led to four hits and six runs for the Brewers, who left Milwaukee after a tenuous win in Game 5 with a 3–2 lead.

Finally, in Game 6, someone played against type. The Cardinals battered Sutton, scoring multiple runs in four separate innings on their way to a 13–1 win. Porter

and Hernandez each homered, and Dane Iorg scored three times and had seven total bases behind Stuper, who allowed one run in a complete-game win.

Game 7 of this always-close series stayed close until the eighth inning when Porter, who would be named World Series MVP, and Steve Braun added insurance runs to Joaquin Andujar's second victory of the series. And so the 1980s were won for speed, defense, Anheuser Busch, and Astroturf.

But what was impressive about Whiteyball wasn't just its World Series championship—it was how often Herzog was able to retool it as personnel changed. When Keith Hernandez left, the Cardinals

Redbird Reference
Willie McGee

The number 51 hasn't technically been retired by the St. Louis Cardinals, but any rookie assigned it will quickly learn, as Bud Smith did in 2001, that to Cardinals fans it might as well be. Few Cardinals have ever been as popular as Willie McGee, who starred through the 1980s as one of the most exciting players on a team designed specifically to be exciting.

Emerging in 1982 first as a vital part of their regular season run and eventually as a breakout postseason star, McGee won two batting titles with the Cardinals and was named the 1985 National League MVP for a season that saw him hit .353 with 18 triples and 56 stolen bases, all career highs.

In 1996 McGee returned to the Cardinals as an ageless fourth outfielder and pinch hitter, one of the only bridges between Whitey Herzog's Cardinals and Tony La Russa's. Which only made sense—in 1990, Whitey Herzog's Cardinals had traded McGee in the first place to Tony La Russa's Oakland Athletics.

replaced their high-average, Gold Glove first baseman with a regular wallbanger, the dangerous Jack Clark. In 1985 they added even more speed when Vince Coleman stole 110 bases in his rookie season. When Bruce Sutter signed with the Braves, the Cardinals found themselves with rookie closer Todd Worrell.

All through the 1980s, stabilized by Ozzie Smith at shortstop, Willie McGee in the outfield, and Bob Forsch in the rotation, the Cardinals managed to find a perfect balance between adhering to their scheme and adjusting their scheme to take advantage of the players they had.

It wasn't until 1990, with the new home run era on the horizon

Behind the Numbers

The Cardinals have led the league in attendance seven times—first in 1892 and most recently in 2000. They first broke three million in attendance in 1987, something they've now done every year since 2004.

and the regulars aging, that the time finally ran out on Whiteyball. But when conditions were right— when Astroturf grew like a weed in National League parks, when outfield fences were out of reach of the average middle infielder—it was hard to find a more perfect strategy.

Opening Day Starts by Position

Position/Player	Opening Day Starts	Years
Catcher		
Ted Simmons	10	1971–80
Yadier Molina	7	2005–11
Del Rice	5	1946, 1949, 1952–54
Darrell Porter		1981–85
First Base		
Jim Bottomley	10	1923–32
Keith Hernandez	9	1975–83
Albert Pujols	8	2004–11
Second Base		
Julian Javier	11	1961–71
Red Schoendienst	10	1947–56
Frankie Frisch	9	1927–29, 1931–36
Third Base		
Ken Boyer	11	1955–65
Ken Reitz	7	1973–75, 1977–80
Whitey Kurowski	6	1943–48
Terry Pendleton		1985–90
Shortstop		
Ozzie Smith	13	1982–88, 1990–95
Marty Marion	9	1940–42, 1944–49
Edgar Renteria	6	1999–2004
Left Field		
Lou Brock	14	1965, 1967–79
Stan Musial	10	1942–43, 1946, 1951–54, 1959, 1961, 1963
Joe Medwick	5	1933, 1935–37, 1939
Vince Coleman		1986–90
Center Field		
Terry Moore	9	1935–42, 1946
Curt Flood	8	1962–69
Jim Edmonds		2000–07
Right Field		
Enos Slaughter	10	1938–42, 1946–47, 1951–53
Stan Musial	5	
George Hendrick		
Pitcher		
Bob Gibson	10	1965, 1967–75
Dizzy Dean	5	1933–37
Chris Carpenter		2005–07, 2010–11

Cardinals Home Stadiums

Ballpark	Seasons
Sportsman's Park	1882–92
Robison Field	1893–1920
Sportsman's Park (Busch Stadium)	1920–66
Busch Memorial Stadium	1966–2005
Busch Stadium (III)	2006-present

Best Single-Season Home Attendance

Year	Total Attendance	Average Attendance Per Game
2007	3,552,180	43,854
2005	3,538,988	43,691
2008	3,432,917	42,382
2006	3,407,104	42,589
2009	3,343,252	41,275
2000	3,336,493	41,191
2010	3,301,218	40,756
1999	3,225,334	40,317
1998	3,195,691	38,972
2001	3,109,578	37,922

Cardinals All-Star Selections

Player	Position	Selections
Stan Musial	OF/1B	24
Ozzie Smith	SS	14
Ken Boyer	3B	11
Enos Slaughter	OF	10
Bob Gibson	SP	9
Albert Pujols	3B/OF/1B	9
Red Schoendienst	2B	9
Marty Marion	SS	8
Bill White	1B	8
Lou Brock	OF	6
Joe Medwick	OF	6
Ted Simmons	C	6
Whitey Kurowski	3B	5
Dizzy Dean	SP	4
Larry Jackson	SP	4
Pepper Martin	3B/OF	4
Willie McGee	OF	4
Johnny Mize	1B	4
Terry Moore	OF	4

Cardinals All-Star Selections

Player	Position	Selections
Scott Rolen	3B	4
Joe Torre	C/3B	4
Steve Carlton	SP	3
Chris Carpenter	SP	3
Walker Cooper	SP	3
Jim Edmonds	OF	3
Curt Flood	OF	3
Frankie Frisch	2B	3
Harvey Haddix	SP	3
Mark McGwire	1B	3
Yadier Molina	C	3
Red Munger	SP	3
Howie Pollet	SP	3
Edgar Renteria	SS	3
Hal Smith	C	3
Lee Smith	RP	3
Joaquin Andujar	SP	2
Harry Brecheen	SP	2
Jack Clark	1B	2
Vince Coleman	OF	2
Ripper Collins	1B	2
Mort Cooper	SP	2
Joe Cunningham	1B	2
David Eckstein	SS	2
Dick Groat	SS	2
George Hendrick	OF/1B	2
Keith Hernandez	1B	2
Matt Holliday	OF	2
Julian Javier	2B	2
Gregg Jefferies	1B	2
Max Lanier	SP	2
Tim McCarver	C	2
Lindy McDaniel	RP	2
Vinegar Bend Mizell	SP	2
Matt Morris	SP	2
Reggie Smith	OF	2
Gerry Staley	SP	2
Bruce Sutter	RP	2
Garry Templeton	SS	2
Lon Warneke	SP	2
Dick Allen	1B	1
Luis Arroyo	SP	1
Red Barrett	SP	1
Lance Berkman	OF	1
Don Blasingame	2B	1
Kent Bottenfield	SP	1

Cardinals All-Star Selections

Player	Position	Selections
Jimmy Brown	2B	1
Orlando Cepeda	1B	1
Royce Clayton	SS	1
Curt Davis	SP	1
Leo Durocher	SS	1
Ryan Franklin	RP	1
Pedro Guerrero	1B	1
Bill Hallahan	SP	1
Tom Henke	RP	1
Tom Herr	2B	1
Jason Isringhausen	RP	1
Ray Jablonski	3B	1
Felix Jose	OF	1
Eddie Kazak	3B	1
Darryl Kile	SP	1
Ray Lankford	OF	1
Ryan Ludwick	OF	1
Stu Martin	2B	1
Bake McBride	OF	1
Lynn McGlothen	SP	1
Wally Moon	OF	1
Ken O'Dea	C	1
Tom Pagnozzi	C	1
Tony Pena	C	1
Ken Reitz	3B	1
Rip Repulski	OF	1
Del Rice	C	1
Lonnie Smith	OF	1
Bob Tewksbury	SP	1
Emil Verban	2B	1
Adam Wainwright	SP	1
Bill Walker	SP	1
Harry Walker	OF	1
Wally Westlake	OF	1
Burgess Whitehead	2B	1
Woody Williams	SP	1
Jimmie Wilson	C	1
Rick Wise	SP	1
Todd Worrell	RP	1

All-Star Games Held in St. Louis

July 9, 1940
8th All-Star Game
National League defeats American League 4–0
Cardinals All-Stars: Terry Moore, Johnny Mize
"Ducky" Joe Medwick, whom the Cardinals had traded to the Brooklyn Dodgers only months earlier, joined Moore and Mize in the National League's starting nine for their 4–0 win. The Cardinals and former Cardinal combined to go 0–7 in the win, which saw Boston outfielder Max West hit a three-run home run off Cleveland phenom Bob Feller. The Browns, visitors in their own ballpark, sent just one player, reserve first baseman George McQuinn, who didn't play.

1948
15th All-Star Game
American League defeats National League 5–2
Cardinals All-Stars: Stan Musial, Enos Slaughter, Harry Brecheen, Marty Marion, Red Schoendienst
A delegation of six Cardinals All-Stars—including starters Musial and Slaughter—couldn't help the National League in its 5–2 loss to the American League, which hosted that season on behalf of the St. Louis Browns.

McQuinn—now playing for the Yankees and starting—had his revenge, going 2–4 and scoring a run, while Browns outfielder Al Zarilla went 0–2 as a reserve.

July 9, 1957
24th All-Star Game
American League defeats National League 6–5
Cardinals All-Stars: Stan Musial, Larry Jackson, Wally Moon, Hal Smith
By 1957, when the last of three All-Star Games at Sportsman's Park was held, Stan Musial—starting that day at first base—had appeared in 14 of the 24 Midsummer Classics that had ever been played. He went 1–3 with a walk, and first-time All-Star Larry Jackson added two scoreless innings, but the National League fell 6–5 despite a three-run rally in the bottom of the ninth.

Former Cardinal Red Schoendienst appeared in his 10th and final All-Star Game—his only one outside the Cardinals organization—as a reserve for the Milwaukee Braves.

All-Star Games held in St. Louis

July 12, 1966
37th All-Star Game
National League defeats American League 2–1 in 10 innings
Cardinals All-Stars: Bob Gibson, Curt Flood, Tim McCarver
On a sweltering July-in-Missouri day—temperatures reached 105 degrees, even outside Busch Memorial Stadium's concrete bowl—the National League won a 2–1 contest in extra innings when Maury Wills drove in McCarver from second on a single.

July 14, 2009
80th All-Star Game
American League defeats National League 4–3
Cardinals All-Stars: Yadier Molina, Albert Pujols, Ryan Franklin
Thirty-two combined All-Star appearances christened the third Busch Stadium's first All-Star Game when Stan Musial delivered the first pitch to President Barack Obama, who threw it to a waiting Albert Pujols.

The National League held the American League to a tie for seven innings, thanks in part to an RBI single from first-time All-Star Molina, but the AL took its seventh consecutive All-Star victory when San Diego closer Heath Bell couldn't get around a Curtis Granderson triple. In a minor Browns-strike-back moment, Orioles outfielder Adam Jones hit the game-winning sacrifice fly.

Chapter 16

Tony La Russa's Cardinals Repaint the Town Red

Managerial Records

Tony La Russa arrived in St. Louis in 1996 with a reputation and a job to do. The reputation was complex. He was the manager behind an Oakland Athletics club that had invented new roles for relief pitchers—and given them ever-smaller fragments of innings to pitch—and at one point attempted to do away with starting pitchers entirely. He was a former Boy Genius with the Chicago White Sox who'd earned a law degree, become a major league manager at 35, and gotten himself fired by Hawk Harrelson.

No manager in the major leagues since Earl Weaver had proven as controversial as La Russa, and few had been as effective.

The job he was hired to do was summarized by his uniform number—win the Cardinals' 10th World Series championship or get fired trying.

The most successful franchise in National League history had fallen on hard times after Whiteyball disintegrated in 1990. The face of the franchise, Ozzie Smith, was a year away from retirement. Attendance was down and Busch Stadium had begun showing its age as teams across the league built gleaming new baseball-only ballparks.

Signing Tony La Russa away from the Athletics was the first sign in years that the Cardinals, under new ownership, were

serious about competing. And for the next 16 years, until La Russa retired following the 2011 season, they did nothing less.

1996: THE WORLD SERIES THAT ALMOST WAS

For one year, all the young talent the old braintrust had been squandering through the early 1990s came together and nearly won the Cardinals a National League pennant. La Russa's first year as Cardinals manager proved to be a volatile combination of controversial issues and feel-good comebacks when Ozzie Smith, coming off the worst season of his career in 1995, found himself backing up 26-year-old Royce Clayton at shortstop.

At the same time, another Whiteyball veteran, 37-year-old Willie McGee, emerged as a vital bench cog behind the powerful outfield bats of Ron Gant, Ray Lankford, and Brian Jordan. The 88-win Cardinals got off to a 3–1 NLCS lead against the perennial-

Behind the Numbers

In the 19th Century, managers were typically also players on the team, and an owner as eccentric and fickle as Chris Von der Ahe was bound to go through plenty of them— including, on three separate occasions, himself.

Behind the Numbers

The Cardinals' two most famous contemporary managers, Tony La Russa and Whitey Herzog, rank 11th and 12th in winning percentage with 2,591 and 1,553 games, respectively.

favorite Atlanta Braves, but a brutal Game 5 loss set them off balance and they never quite recovered. In Game 7, Donovan Osborne failed to get out of the first inning, and the Braves rolled to the World Series by a score of 15–0.

The team wouldn't return to the postseason under La Russa until 2000 when the seeds of the Cardinals' first pennant winners since 1987 were finally sewn.

2002: TRAGEDY AND NEAR-TRIUMPH

One of the most impressive and unfortunate discoveries about Tony La Russa in his tenure with the Cardinals was his ability to deal with tragedy, which seemed to strike the Cardinals too frequently during his tenure. In 2002 ace starter Darryl Kile was found dead in his hotel room during a weekend series in Chicago.

The Cardinals, with an improvised rotation and DK57 shoulder patches, played the rest of the season in Kile's honor, recovering from an early tailspin to go 21–6 in September before

Behind the Numbers

On the death of her uncle, Stanley Robison, Helene Hathaway Britton inherited a baseball team and a mantle—the first female owner of a baseball franchise. Surprisingly for baseball fans who expected her to give up control immediately, she did something with both pieces of her inheritance. At one point she even went head to head with Roger Bresnahan, the Cardinals' famously rough-and-tumble manager, firing him after he told her no woman could tell him how to run a baseball game.

That made Bresnahan the first manager to learn that a woman could tell him how to run a baseball game because she held the purse strings.

Tony La Russa's Bullpen Management in a Postseason Nutshell

In 2011, with the chance to represent the National League in the World Series on the line, the Cardinals' rotation suddenly and permanently collapsed.

Jaime Garcia came first—the Brewers put two runs on him to start and added six more in a brutal fifth that started with a single, two doubles, and a home run, and things got worse from there.

La Russa extrapolated, from that outing, some of the quickest hooks ever seen outside a World Series Game 7. In Game 2 Edwin Jackson was removed with two outs in the fifth inning, a runner on first base, and a three-run lead. To protect what eventually became a series-tying 12–3 lead, La Russa deployed six relievers.

What had long been a Tony La Russa running joke was now reality. Starters had been usurped by an unrelenting stream of single-use relief pitchers, and it was somehow working. Even Chris Carpenter wasn't immune; after five shaky but serviceable innings in Game 3, he was replaced by four more relievers. In his second appearance Garcia allowed one fifth-inning run before being pulled with a 4–1 lead. By the time the Cardinals were in a position to clinch in Game 6, they required six relievers in a game that saw them score nine runs in the first three innings.

Fittingly, Jason Motte, the leader of the pack, was on the mound for the last out, striking out Mark Kotsay on three pitches. In the end the Cardinals' relievers had thrown more innings than their starters in those six games, fulfilling an end-of-the-world La Russa prophecy dating back 30 years.

losing in the NLCS against the San Francisco Giants.

2004: PENNANT PARALYSIS

On a pure talent basis, it would be harder to find a better Cardinals team than the one Tony La Russa managed to 105 wins in 2004. Albert Pujols, Jim Edmonds, and Scott Rolen combined that year to hit 122 homers and drive in 358 runs. And by the time the Cardinals won their classic NLCS showdown with the Houston Astros, that core was supplemented by Larry Walker, who was acquired in midseason for pitching prospects.

But that team had the misfortune of running into the 2004 Boston Red Sox, who were in the process

Behind the Numbers

Roger Connor, who at .178 holds the Cardinals' all-time record for lowest winning percentage for a manager, is better known for being the last player to hold the record for career home runs before Babe Ruth changed baseball. Connor hit 138 between 1880 and 1897, leading the major leagues with 14 in 1890.

of winning their first World Series since Babe Ruth was a going concern. A brutal four-game sweep left lingering questions in St. Louis about La Russa's ability to win in the postseason—he had led

Tony La Russa's Smooth Lucky Charm

Tony La Russa's famous friends usually show up to spring training, where you're liable to see Bobby Knight, Bill Parcells, or some other star in the coaching constellation lecturing non-roster invitees or hitting fungoes. But it was his friendship with a guitar hero that precipitated the Cardinals' (and the coach's) last World Series run.

On September 6, La Russa abruptly canceled his postgame press conference to exercise his backstage pass at Carlos Santana's concert at the Fox Theater. That night La Russa played the maracas onstage and got, for his troubles, Santana's necklace. La Russa wore it for the rest of the regular season—the Cardinals went 14–5—and everything else rapidly became history.

According to Derrick Goold of the *Post-Dispatch*, Tony La Russa denied it was a good luck charm. "It's just a necklace," he said. "It's a cool gift." But some at the scene report that Santana told La Russa that he, and the Cardinals, needed it more than the guitarist.

similarly dominant Athletics teams to similar defeats in 1988 and 1990.

2006: Champions by Accident

The 2006 Cardinals spent most of their regular season trying desperately to avoid total collapse, and entered the postseason that year, as a result, in a state of partial collapse. Injuries and age had diminished the 2004 club's powerful batting order, while the pitching staff was heavily dependent on just two starters who finished with ERAs under 5.06.

If being a manager is about working with limited resources, what followed was La Russa's finest hour. Scott Spiezio, who'd hit .061 in 2005, filled in across the diamond while slugging .496. Chris Duncan, who'd been blocked in the minor leagues by Albert Pujols, was sent to lumber around the outfield because the Cardinals suddenly couldn't do without his bat.

In the rotation, La Russa cobbled together a postseason staff out of his two anchors, Chris Carpenter and Jeff Suppan; a struggling trade acquisition, Jeff Weaver; and an inconsistent rookie, Anthony Reyes. When his closer faltered he replaced him with a rotation prospect, Adam Wainwright, who had ended up in the bullpen because they didn't have any place to put him.

Behind the Numbers

With World War II confusing baseball's landscape by the season, Billy Southworth led the Cardinals to two World Series championships and three National League pennants in five seasons as St. Louis' wartime manager. As the Cardinals' young player-manager in 1929, Southworth struggled to create discipline and was dismissed.

After dealing with the death of his wife and problems with alcoholism, Southworth returned to the Cardinals in 1940 and turned around a young Cardinals team almost immediately, climbing into the first division in 1940 and into the National League pennant race in 1941. By 1942, led by young players like Stan Musial and Marty Marion, the Cardinals had won the first of three consecutive pennants.

By the time the World Series was over and Tony La Russa had finally earned that 10th World Series championship in his 11th season with the club, the inconsistent rookie had nearly thrown a shutout in Game 1, and the struggling trade acquisition had clinched the series in Game 5, thanks in part to a save from the rotation prospect.

Won-Lost Records by Manager

Years	Manager	W–L
1882	Ned Cuthbert	37–43
1883	Ted Sullivan	53–26
1883–89, 1891	Charlie Comiskey	563–273
1884	Jimmy Williams	51–33
1890	Chief Roseman	7–8
1890	Tommy McCarthy	15–12
1890	John Kerins	9–8
1890	Joe Gerhart	20–16
1890	Count Campau	27–14
1892	Cub Stricker	6–17
1892	George Gore	6–9
1892	Jack Glasscock	1–3
1892	Jack Crooks	27–33
1892	Bob Caruthers	16–32
1893	Bill Watkins	57–75
1894	Doggie Miller	56–76
1895, 1896, 1897	Chris Von der Ahe	3–14
1895	Joe Quinn	11–28
1895	Lou Phelan	11–30
1895	Al Buckenberger	16–34
1896	Arlie Latham	0–3
1896, 1897	Tommy Dowd	31–60
1896	Harry Diddlebock	7–10
1896	Roger Connor	8–37
1897	Hugh Nicol	8–32
1897	Bill Hallman	13–36
1898	Tim Hurst	39–111
1899–1900	Patsy Tebeau	126–117
1900	Louis Heilbroner	23–25
1901–03	Patsy Donovan	175–236
1904–05	Kid Nichols	80–88
1905	Stan Robison	19–31
1905	Jimmy Burke	34–56
1906–08	John McCloskey	34–56
1909–12	Roger Bresnahan	255–352
1913–17	Miller Huggins	346–415
1918	Jack Hendricks	51–58
1919–25	Branch Rickey	458–485
1925–26	Rogers Hornsby	153–116
1927	Bob O'Farrell	92–61
1928–29	Bill McKechnie	129–88
1929–33	Gabby Street	312–242
1933–38	Frankie Frisch	458–354
1938, 1940	Mike Gonzalez	9–13
1939–40	Ray Blades	106–85
1929, 1940–45	Billy Southworth	620–346

Won-Lost Records by Manager

Years	Manager	W–L
1946–50	Eddie Dyer	446–325
1951	Marty Marion	81–73
1952–55	Eddie Stanky	260–238
1956–58	Fred Hutchinson	232–220
1958	Stan Hack	3–7
1959–61	Solly Hemus	190–192
1961–64	John Keane	317–249
1965–76, 1980, 1990	Red Schoendienst	1,041–955
1977–78	Vernon Rapp	89–90
1978–80	Ken Boyer	166–190
1978, 1980	Jack Krol	1–2
1980–90	Whitey Herzog	822–728
1990–95	Joe Torre	351–354
1995	Mike Jorgensen	42–54
1996–2011	Tony La Russa	1,408–1,182

Redbird Reference

Branch Rickey

The St. Louis Cardinals owe their unparalleled success in the National League to all kinds of people, from players to owners to the first guy to buy a beer and a hot dog at Chris Von der Ahe's ballpark in the 1880s. But for the mechanisms that made the Cardinals one of the most dominant teams in the history of baseball—and the players they produced—St. Louis owes Branch Rickey, the most dynamic, instrumental executive who ever lived.

Any one of the things he revolutionized would have made him a Hall of Famer—the list itself is almost too long to fit into one capsule. He saw the promise of sabermetric analysis 50 years before *Moneyball*, and he helped define modern spring training.

He created the modern farm system—he strung together innumerable minor league teams into something recognizable today as the farm; developing Dizzy Dean, Joe Medwick, Stan Musial, Marty Marion, Enos Slaughter, Pepper Martin—two generations of Cardinals stars, from the Gashouse Gang right into the 1950s.

There was also, later on, that matter of signing Jackie Robinson and breaking the color barrier. All of Rickey's achievements can be most neatly summarized by this one fact. Before Branch Rickey, people didn't talk about general managers. After Branch Rickey, they did.

World Series Championships by Manager

Rank	Manager	Championships	Years
1.	Billy Southworth	2	1942, 1944
	Tony La Russa	2	2006, 2011
3.	Rogers Hornsby	1	1926
	Gabby Street	1	1931
	Frankie Frisch	1	1934
	Eddie Dyer	1	1946
	John Keane	1	1964
	Red Schoendienst	1	1967
	Whitey Herzog	1	1982

Manager of the Year Awards

Year	Manager	Season Record
1985	Whitey Herzog	101–61
2002	Tony La Russa	97–65

Games Managed

Rank	Manager	Games	Years
1.	Tony La Russa	2,591	1996–2011
2.	Red Schoendienst	1,999	1965–76, 1980, 1990
3.	Whitey Herzog	1,553	1980–90
4.	Billy Southworth	981	1929, 1940–45
5.	Branch Rickey	947	1919–25
6.	Charlie Comiskey	852	1883–89, 1891
7.	Frankie Frisch	822	1933–38
8.	Eddie Dyer	777	1946–50
9.	Miller Huggins	774	1913–17
10.	Joe Torre	706	1990–95

Timeline of Cardinals Owners

Chris Von der Ahe	1882–98
Frank and Stanley Robison	1899–10
Helene Hathaway Britton	1911–16
Sam Breadon	1917–47
Fred Saigh and Robert Hannegan	1948
Fred Saigh	1949–52
Gussie Busch	1953–89
Anheuser-Busch	1989–96
Bill DeWitt Jr.	1996–present

Most Wins by a Manager

Rank	Manager	W–L	Years
1.	Tony La Russa	1,408–1,182	1996–2011
2.	Red Schoendienst	1,041–955	1965–76, 1980, 1990
3.	Whitey Herzog	822–728	1980–90
4.	Billy Southworth	620–346	1929, 1940–45
5.	Charlie Comiskey	563–273	1883–89, 1891
6.	Branch Rickey	458–485	1919–25
7.	Frankie Frisch	458–354	1933–38
8.	Eddie Dyer	446–325	1946–50
9.	Joe Torre	351–354	1990–95
10.	Miller Huggins	346–415	1913–17

Winning Percentage by Manager

Rank	Manager	W–L	Winning Percentage
1.	Charlie Comiskey	563–273	.673
2.	Billy Southworth	620–346	.642
3.	Bob O'Farrell	92–61	.601
4.	Bill McKechnie	129–88	.594
5.	Eddie Dyer	446–325	.578
6.	Rogers Hornsby	153–116	.569
7.	Frankie Frisch	428–354	.564
8.	Gabby Street	312–242	.563
9.	John Keane	317–249	.560
10.	Ray Blades	106–85	.555

Timeline of Cardinals General Managers

Branch Rickey	1919–42
William Walsingham Jr.	1942–53
Richard A. Meyer	1953–55
Frank Lane	1955–57
Bing Devine	1957–64
Bob Howsam	1964–66
Stan Musial	1967
Bing Devine	1967–78
John Claiborne	1978–80
Whitey Herzog	1980–82
Joe McDonald	1982–84
Dal Maxvill	1984–94
Walt Jocketty	1994–2007
John Mozeliak	2007–present

First Amateur Draft Picks by Year

Year	Player	Position	Cardinals Career
1965	Joe DiFabio	RHP	n/a
1966	Leron Lee	INF	1969–71
1967	Ted Simmons	C	1968–80
1968	Butch Hairston	OF	n/a
1969	Charles Minott	LHP	n/a
1970	Jim Browning	RHP	n/a
1971	Ed Kurpiel	1B	n/a
1972	Dan Larson	RHP	n/a
1973	Joe Edelen	RHP	1981
1974	Garry Templeton	SS	1976–81
1975	David Johnson	LHP	n/a
1976	Leon Durham	1B	1980, 1989
1977	Terry Kennedy	C	1978–80
1978	Bob Hicks	1B	n/a
1979	Andy Van Slyke	OF	1983–86
1980	Donald Collins	RHP	n/a
1981	Bob Meacham	SS	n/a
1982	Todd Worrell	RHP	1985–89
1983	Jim Lindeman	OF	1986–89
1984	Mike Dunne	RHP	n/a
1985	Joe Magrane	LHP	1987–90, 1992–93
1986	Luis Alicea	2B	1988, 1991–94, 1996
1987	Cris Carpenter	RHP	1988–92
1988	Brad Duvall	RHP	n/a
1989	Paul Coleman	OF	n/a
1990	Donovan Osborne	LHP	1992–93, 1995–99
1991	Dmitri Young	1B	1996–97
1992	Sean Lowe	RHP	1997–98
1993	Alan Benes	RHP	1995–97, 1999–2001
1994	Bret Wagner	LHP	n/a
1995	Matt Morris	RHP	1997–98, 2000–05
1996	Braden Looper	RHP	1998, 2006–08
1997	Adam Kennedy	2B	1999, 2007–08
1998	J.D. Drew	OF	1998–2003
1999	Chance Caple	RHP	n/a
2000	Shaun Boyd	2B/OF	n/a
2001	Justin Pope	RHP	n/a
2002	Calvin Hayes	SS	n/a
2003	Daric Barton	C	n/a
2004	Chris Lambert	RHP	n/a
2005	Colby Rasmus	CF	2009–11
2006	Adam Ottavino	RHP	2010
2007	Pete Kozma	SS	2011
2008	Brett Wallace	1B	n/a
2009	Shelby Miller	RHP	n/a
2010	Zack Cox	3B	n/a
2011	Kolten Wong	2B	n/a

Redbird Reference

Jim Edmonds

During Walt Jocketty's run as General Manager between 1994 and 2007, the Cardinals tended to get more value out of trading their first-round draft picks than actually starting them. Never was that more true than in 2000 when the Cardinals, just before the start of then season, packaged top second-base prospect Adam Kennedy and 18-game winner Kent Bottenfield into a trade for Anaheim Angels center fielder Jim Edmonds.

Edmonds had been an exciting, inconsistent player for the Angels, but an injury-plagued 1999 season led to rumors about his clubhouse presence, and Jocketty, sensing a chance to buy low, made a bet that the rumors were just that.

He'd never been more right. Edmonds, originally given the tongue-in-cheek nickname of "Hollywood" for his theatrical acrobatics in center, became so popular in St. Louis that fans had trouble determining in the end whether he was more a "Jimmy Baseball" or a "Jimmy Ballgame." In the clubhouse he proved a vocal leader—too vocal, if anything—rather than a malingerer.

And on the field he put together one of the best runs any center fielder has ever had. Already 30 in 2000, his next six seasons saw him develop into one of the strongest hitters in baseball. To go with six Gold Gloves, Edmonds averaged, between 2000 and 2005, 35 home runs, 98 RBIs, 92 walks, and 100 runs scored.

Underrated even in his prime, Edmonds is a deserving and unlikely Hall of Fame candidate. But Cardinals will have his heroic performances in the 2004 NLCS to remember him by—both his 12th-inning walkoff home run in Game 6, which left Edmonds fist-pumping in disbelief and Houston Astros fans just in disbelief, and his famous Game 7 catch, which saw all his defensive talents coalesce in one perfect route and one unbelievable dive.

CHAPTER 17

THE ST. LOUIS CARDINALS CHARGE TO THE WORLD SERIES IN 2011
World Series Records, 2011 Results

Nobody knows quite how improbable the Cardinals' 2011 run to their 11th World Series championship was better than Tyler Greene. On August 25, with the Cardinals 10 games out of first place in the National League Central, general manager John Mozeliak told the *St. Louis Post-Dispatch* that he and manager Tony La Russa had met with the idea that Greene, the Cardinals' fleet-footed, inconsistent young shortstop, would play more down the stretch so that the Cardinals could see what they had in him for 2012.

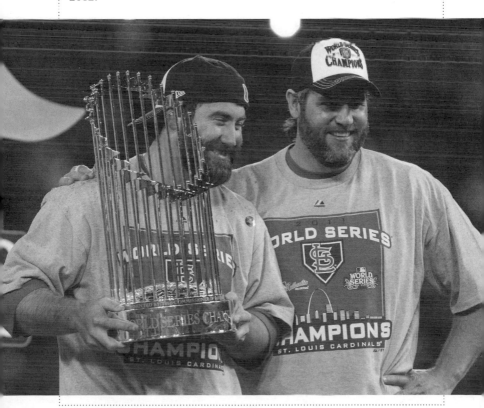

For a few days it looked like Greene would get his first chance to play every day when rosters expanded that September. As things turned out, he wouldn't get a single start that month because while that article sat on newsstands, the Cardinals won an 8–4 game against the Pirates.

That game anticipated much of the rest of their season, though nobody could have known it at the time. First, the moves they'd made with an eye toward the playoffs seemed to falter all at once—trade-deadline acquisition Edwin Jackson allowed four runs to give the Pirates a bitter 4–3 lead in the fourth inning, thanks to sloppy play on defense and Jackson's poor command.

An inning later, things turned around. David Freese hit a bases-loaded single down the right field line, scoring Allen Craig and Albert Pujols and putting the Cardinals back on top. Jackson stayed on top of the Pirates, the Cardinals' newly revised bullpen proved unhittable, and the Cardinals left Busch Stadium with a win after a depressing three-game sweep at the hands of the Dodgers earlier that week.

At the time it didn't mean much—the Cardinals gained half a game on the Brewers with little more than 30 to go. They'd just lost seven of their last nine, and most fans had already begun looking forward to the September

call-ups and the Hot Stove League.

But the Cardinals kept winning. They won three out of four against Pittsburgh and swept Milwaukee, and by the time they'd taken three straight games against the Atlanta Braves on September 11, fans realized there was one more way for these Cardinals— these incredibly frustrating, deeply unsatisfying, remarkably inconsistent Cardinals—to frustrate expectations and reach the postseason berth that had seemed not even worth considering earlier. As late as September 12, Las Vegas offered 999-to-1 odds, which earned one wildly confident Cardinals fan a cool $125,000 come October.

They could win the Wild Card—on September 1, the Cardinals had been even further back of the heavily favored Braves than they were of the Brewers. But on the 11th the Cardinals were 4½ back, with 16 games to go. It would take the Braves' help, but the Cardinals had given themselves their first legitimate shot at the postseason since days after they'd rebuilt their 25-man roster for a playoff push.

So Rafael Furcal stayed in the lineup; Edwin Jackson stayed in the rotation; Marc Rzepczynski, Octavio Dotel, Kyle McClellan, Arthur Rhodes, and the rest of the refashioned bullpen came in with no regard for 2012. After a week of preparations for waiting 'til next

David Freese's Charmed Playoff Run

National League Division Series: St. Louis Cardinals defeat Philadelphia Phillies 3 games to 2

Date	Result	AB	R	H	2B	3B	HR	RBI	WPA
10/1/11	L, 6–11	3	0	0	0	0	0	0	-0.04
10/2/11	W, 5–4	4	0	1	1	0	0	0	-0.05
10/4/11	L, 2–3	5	0	1	0	0	0	1	-0.1
10/5/11	W, 5–3	3	1	2	1	0	1	4	0.38
10/7/11	W, 1–0	3	0	1	0	0	0	0	-0.04

G	AB	R	H	2B	3B	HR	RBI	SB	BB	SO	AVG	OBP	SLG
5	18	1	5	2	0	1	5	0	0	9	.278	.278	.556

National League Championship Series: St. Louis Cardinals defeat Milwaukee Brewers 4 games to 2

Date	Result	AB	R	H	2B	3B	HR	RBI	WPA
10/9/11	L, 6–9	3	1	1	0	0	1	3	0.27
10/10/11	W, 12–3	5	1	2	0	0	1	2	-0.02
10/12/11	W, 4–3	4	0	3	2	0	0	1	0.05
10/13/11	L, 2–4	4	0	2	0	0	0	0	0.00
10/14/11	W, 7–1	4	2	1	0	0	0	0	0.05
10/16/11	W, 12–6	4	3	3	1	0	1	3	0.31

G	AB	R	H	2B	3B	HR	RBI	SB	BB	SO	AVG	OBP	SLG
6	22	7	12	3	0	3	9	0	2	2	.545	.600	1.091

2012 World Series: St. Louis Cardinals defeat Texas Rangers 4 games to 3

Date	Result	AB	R	H	2B	3B	HR	RBI	WPA
10/19/11	W, 3–2	2	1	1	0	0	0	0	0.13
10/20/11	L, 1–2	3	1	1	0	0	0	0	-0.02
10/22/11	W, 16–7	4	1	2	1	0	0	2	0.14
10/23/11	L, 0–4	3	0	0	0	0	0	0	-0.16
10/24/11	L, 2–4	4	0	1	0	0	0	0	-0.17
10/16/11	W, 10–9	5	1	2	0	1	1	3	0.97
10/28/11	W, 6–2	2	0	1	1	0	0	2	0.20

G	AB	R	H	2B	3B	HR	RBI	SB	BB	SO	AVG	OBP	SLG
7	23	4	8	3	1	1	7	0	5	3	.348	.464	.696

Playoff Totals

G	AB	R	H	2B	3B	HR	RBI	SB	BB	SO	AVG	OBP	SLG
18	63	12	25	8	1	5	21	0	7	14	.397	.465	.794

year, the Cardinals wrapped Tyler
Greene back up in cellophane,
left the tags on Matt Carpenter,
and paid up the deposit on their
allotment of spraying-champagne.

So the varsity Cardinals kept
playing, and the Braves, for their
part, kept losing. Albert Pujols'
return to being Albert Pujols—he'd
hit .355 in September—powered
the offense, while the rotation
had its best month of the season.
Kyle Lohse, who'd struggled all
summer, was 2–0 with a 1.37
ERA; Chris Carpenter and Jaime
Garcia combined to win six games
without a loss.

On September 26, one
game behind the Braves in the
Wild Card, the Cardinals lost a
crushing 10-inning contest to
the Astros when former Houston
closer Dotel mishandled a bunt
in front of home plate. But the
Braves couldn't pull away, losing
a game to Philadelphia when the
Phillies—despite clinching long
before—brought out ace Cliff Lee
to predictable effect.

The Cardinals, who'd used up
somewhat more than nine lives
already, seemed reenergized. Over
the next two days, they outscored
the hapless Astros 21–6 thanks to
big days from surprise contributors
Allen Craig, Skip Schumaker, and
Nick Punto, forcing nothing less
than a play-in game if the Braves
could win one of their last two
against the Phillies. But Atlanta's
first game was a 7–1 walkover, and

their second, on a September 28
in which nearly every postseason
race seemed to come down to
late-innings heroics, saw them lose
a 13-inning heartbreaker when
another former Astro, Hunter
Pence, singled up the middle to
break a 3–3 tie.

It was true, somehow—the
Cardinals were going to the
postseason, and they'd be doing
it against those same Phillies, the
prohibitive World Series favorites
all season.

Everyone knew about the
Phillies' credentials—one of the
greatest pitching rotations ever
assembled, an offense filled with
big names, a 102-win regular
season—but all the baseball world
knew about the Cardinals was
the bad news they'd ridden in on.
Adam Wainwright had missed the
entire season after tearing an elbow
ligament; Albert Pujols had the
first "down" season of his career.

For all that, St. Louis—city and
team—seemed to float into the
National League Division Series on
a house-money high. Just a month
earlier, nobody had expected
anything save for the distinct
pleasure of watching Tyler Greene
run the bases; after one of the most
exhilarating regular season finishes
in recent memory, Cardinals fans
seemed happy to just see what
happened.

What happened, luckily
enough, was just as exhilarating.
Game 1 was an abbreviated look

at what everyone expected. Roy Halladay looked outstanding on full rest after Lance Berkman got to him. But Lohse, pressed into service because Carpenter's services had been required in the regular season, fell apart after five solid innings. Problems from the bullpen led to an 11–6 loss and a host of TV-bound St. Louis fans telling each other, "Well, it's been a great season no matter what."

But the Cardinals, their backs against the wall as usual, weren't about to settle for it having been a great season. The first inkling of the bullpen's upcoming virtuoso performance came in Game 2 when Carpenter faltered on three days' rest and was picked up by six scoreless relief innings.

In the meantime, the Cardinals' offense fought back against Cliff Lee, the second of the Phillies' famous starters. Twice the bottom of the order came through—Yadier Molina, Ryan Theriot, and Jon Jay accounted for the first of the Cardinals' three runs in the fourth, with Jay returning in the sixth to score Theriot again and tie the game. In the seventh Allen Craig led off with a triple deep to center field, misplayed by Shane

Redbird Reference

Roger Maris

By the time Roger Maris reached St. Louis, he'd been drummed out of New York—where he'd never be Mickey Mantle, let alone Babe Ruth—and beset by injuries that had sapped him of his famous power and his ability to stay in the lineup. But the man who had struggled to ingratiate himself with fans while hitting 61 home runs in 1961 proved immediately popular in St Louis, where he would hit just 14 in 225 games.

What had seemed distant and stand-offish to the loquacious Yankees media fit Maris' new Midwestern fanbase just right, and when he drove in seven of the Cardinals' 17 runs in their 1967 World Series win over the Boston Red Sox, he had made it—he'd be a True Cardinal forever.

Of course, beating the Red Sox probably made him more popular than he'd ever been in Yankees circles, too.

Contemporary Comparo: In 2004 the Cardinals acquired Larry Walker, another injury-prone, aging superstar who proceeded to stabilize right field on offense and defense and even hit well in the World Series against the Red Sox. Unfortunately, the outcome wasn't quite as perfect.

Victorino, to set up an entirely conventional game-winner when Albert Pujols lined Lee's first pitch over the infielders for their fifth run.

Just as in August, all the pieces of the Cardinals' historical run were there in miniature in Game 2—the constant rallies from unexpected places, the remarkable bullpen work, and the refusal to concede defeat against unpleasant odds.

But it was difficult to see the trees for the forest at the time—after the travel day, the Cardinals lost a 3–2 nailbiter at Busch Stadium when Cole Hamels topped Garcia in a duel of young left-handers. The next day, with Jackson matched evenly with Roy Oswalt, the Cardinals and their fans had one consolation—their ace was still up their sleeve. Chris Carpenter awaited on full rest if the Cardinals could get to the shakiest of the Phillies' four-of-a-kind.

That was of little use after Jackson allowed them a home run short of the cycle in the top of the first inning. Jimmy Rollins led off with a ground-rule double, which Chase Utley followed up with a triple and Hunter Pence capped with a single. But if it hadn't already become evident, the Cardinals' offense was no longer the rusty mechanism of July and August. Berkman doubled off his long-time teammate in the bottom of the inning to score a run, and in

the fifth inning David Freese made his first appearance in the history books, doubling down the line to put the Cardinals ahead for good.

The stage had been set for a Game 5 matchup between the Cardinals' only ace standing and the Phillies' ace-of-aces, Roy Halladay, a matchup that was rapidly sliced into narrative-ready pieces by a hungry media. Not only were Carpenter and Halladay number-one starters, they were former Blue Jays; not only were they former Blue Jays, they were close friends and fishing buddies who'd come up at the same time as future superstars who'd taken long detours on their way there.

Halladay, in the midst of an incredible 10-year run and as good as he'd ever been, was a known quantity. It was Carpenter—coming off a season that had been a struggle from the start after a disastrous outing on three days' rest—who would determine the outcome of the game.

And the Carpenter the world saw was spectacular. For the second game in a row, the Cardinals got on top of Halladay in the top of the first inning when Rafael Furcal tripled and Skip Schumaker, with two strikes, pulled a double over Howard's head for the first run of the night. And for the second game in a row, that lead felt strangely ominous—despite earning every advantage, the offense was unable to expand that one-run lead.

Pujols reached second on a wild pitch, and Berkman reached on an exceedingly rare catcher's interference call. But neither could score, and it was obvious immediately that Halladay's first-inning jitters were again an anomaly. One run was all the Cardinals would get, and they were lucky to have it.

So it was that with a nervous feeling in the pit of their collective stomach that Cardinals fans across the country watched Carpenter take apart the Phillies with ruthless efficiency. Both pitchers induced weak grounder after weak grounder, allowing just one runner a piece to reach third base, and the game moved so quickly that even with the postseason's profusion of commercial breaks, just over two hours had passed when the Cardinals' bats were blown away again and Chris Carpenter returned to the mound, 102 pitches on his ragged arm and the middle of the Phillies' order strung on a dangerous line from the batter's box to the dugout.

Carpenter had been helped out by his newly provisioned defense twice in the late innings; Rafael Furcal had made a beautiful dive and had to augment his infamous arm with a spin-move, while oft-injured utility man Nick Punto had changed course on a ball deflected by Carpenter in time to record the last out with a runner on first. But nobody in Citizens

Remember When...

Twitter-related *schadenfreude* reached an all-time high in St. Louis after the NLCS thanks to a particularly ironic tweet from Brewers outfielder Nyjer Morgan (aka @TheRealTPlush) circa September 7, as the Cardinals' rally was in progress. It read, in full: "Where still n 1st and I hope those crying birds injoy watching tha Crew in tha Playoffs!!! Aaaaahhhhh!!!"

Morgan had earlier earned Twitter fame for repeatedly calling Albert Pujols "Alberta." Unsurprisingly, most of its 100+ retweets came after the Cardinals' NLCS win.

Bank Park that night had any doubt he'd go back out for the ninth inning, least of all Tony La Russa, even after Chase Utley came a yardstick away from a home run for the second time.

With that one precarious out, Carpenter settled again—Pence grounded weakly to third base, Howard slapped a 2–2 pitch to Punto, and the Cardinals had beaten the Phillies and taken their first step toward their second totally inexplicable World Series appearance in six years.

For their trouble, the Cardinals drew their never-quite-vanquished regular-season nemesis, the Milwaukee Brewers. It was the

Brewers' unstoppable summer, in which they'd won 19 games in 21 tries right as the Cardinals were making what was supposed to be their last playoff push, that had made all the hand-wringing and that improbable September necessary. They were coming off a team-of-destiny Game 5 of their own, too—they'd taken 10 innings to dispatch the Arizona Diamondbacks after losing both games in Phoenix thanks to a walkoff single from mustache-twirling pro-wrestling-style-heel Nyjer Morgan.

As it turned out, though, the NL Central showdown wouldn't be about Nyjer Morgan, his feud with Albert Pujols, or Chris Carpenter's brilliant performance. It would be about... relief pitching.

And the Cardinals had made the World Series on their third pennant in Tony La Russa's 16-year odyssey as manager of the Cardinals. While the bullpen's complete takeover of the pitching duties was dominating coverage of the National League champions, David Freese, the Cardinals' injury-prone third baseman, had run off with the NLCS MVP trophy, putting together one of the best postseason series any Cardinal has had since Lou Brock took his last catcher's scalp.

He'd driven in nine runs, including the three-run homer that had driven Game 6 starter Shaun Marcum from the series finale, and hit .545, flashing the power that had mostly been absent since he'd come over from San Diego as a minor league slugger a little too old for his league.

In the World Series the Cardinals would meet one last heavily favored division-winner, the back-to-back American League champion Texas Rangers. With a rotation reminiscent, in its absurd stability, of the 2004 Cardinals' staff sans the unfortunate Chris Carpenter injury, they'd ridden big offensive seasons from new acquisitions Adrian Beltre and Mike Napoli into an unconventionally balanced season for the stereotypically hulking Rangers.

Which was not to say they didn't also have a great offense—for the third time in a row, the Cardinals had run into a team that was like them in most superficial ways, only better by almost every statistical measure. On their side of the tale of the tape, the Cardinals had home-field advantage, courtesy of the recently vanquished Prince Fielder, who'd homered off Rangers ace C.J. Wilson to put the National League on top; Tony La Russa, who had looked almost clairvoyant in his choice of relief pitcher against the Brewers; and their strange ability, through the first two series, to win in unpleasant and unlikely ways.

Thanks to that first advantage, the Cardinals didn't need the third one to win Game 1—Busch Stadium quieted both offenses, and Carpenter, shaky but effective after dealing with a sore arm through the NLCS, got by Wilson thanks to a pinch-hit RBI from Allen Craig.

After Carpenter's six innings—and after Craig's single laid waste to Alexi Ogando, the Rangers' own bullpen talisman following a dominant ALCS performance—Tony La Russa went back to the relievers that had earned him the pennant. He punched in what had, by then, become the usual. Five relievers, three righties and both lefties, retired nine batters and allowed two baserunners to

Torty Craig's Twitter Fame

Animals are unofficially barred from winning Most Valuable Player awards, but Torty Craig, the shelled hero of the 2011 Cardinals, will be remembered as long as people are talking in 140-character bursts.

It started, as many online Cardinals memes did in 2011, with an off-hand comment from the Cardinals' broadcasting booth. In September, when the Cardinals had begun their surreal run for a postseason berth, reporter Jim Hayes passed along some interesting information. When white-hot second-year outfielder Allen Craig was up at the plate, the dugout was now imploring him to "Do it for Torty!" where "it" was get a hit, drive in a run, or draw a crucial walk, and "Torty" was the adorably curt name of Craig's five-year-old pet turtle.

It was the team mantra for a few weeks, but after that report bubbled up on the Internet it became the online fanbase's rally cry for the rest of the postseason. Later that month, an anonymous fan of the Cardinals and Alfred, Lord Tennyson began @TortyCraig, a Twitter account—followed by more than 20,000 fans—that purported to detail the adventures of the Cardinals on their way to the postseason all the way through to the moments after the parade, when a tearful Tony La Russa had to tell our reptilian clubhouse reporter that, despite his protestations, "[Commissioner] Selig has issued a ban on talking animals in the clubhouse."

Other Twitter accounts followed—one for Jason Motte's talking glove, and another for the Rally Squirrel, Busch Stadium's pitch-disrupting pet—but @TortyCraig, with its long tales of mild clubhouse debauchery, perfectly captured the loose, unrehearsed feeling of the postseason run and the championship, both for the players it fictionalized and the fans who followed along.

save Carpenter's third win of the postseason.

If Game 1 had been emblematic of all the Cardinals' successes in the postseason so far, Game 2 was a worrying example of their inadequacies. Jaime Garcia's seven scoreless innings gave them their best start since Carpenter had outdueled Halladay in Philadelphia, but the Cardinals could put just one run on struggling Rangers starter Colby Lewis when Craig burned Ogando for the second night in a row.

The usual suspects came out for the eighth inning—Fernando Salas and Marc Rzepczynski, making their sixth and 10th appearances of the postseason—but in the ninth inning, the bullpen showed its first cracks since the NLDS. Motte, who'd finally become the shutdown closer in everything but name, allowed the first two baserunners he saw to reach second and third, and rather than stick with his best reliever, La Russa tried once more to play the matchups as he had in Milwaukee.

Out came a shaky-looking Arthur Rhodes to face Josh Hamilton, whose own shakiness led to immediate questions about the move. Hamilton, the 2010 MVP, was typically one of the most dangerous left-handers in baseball. But a groin injury had held him powerless in recent weeks, and he'd looked off-balance at best in two World Series games. Nevertheless,

he had just enough in him to slap a lifeless pitch from Rhodes into right field, scoring the tying run and stranding the Cardinals without their best reliever to face the next two right-handers in the Rangers lineup. Lance Lynn, who came in to face Mike Young in Motte's absence, allowed a second sacrifice fly, and that was all Rangers closer Neftali Feliz needed—the Series would go to the Ballpark in Arlington tied at 1.

Citizens Bank Park in Philadelphia and Miller Park in Milwaukee were both nominally hitters' parks, but the Ballpark in Arlington was the real deal, perhaps the most home run friendly in the major leagues. After winning on the strength of their starting pitching in the NLDS and the resilience of their bullpen in the NLCS, the Cardinals, who had led the National League in runs scored in the regular season, would have to adapt fully to American League ball and show off the bats to win in Texas.

More than the 2006 or 2004 pennant-winners, these Cardinals were lucky enough to be perfectly suited to AL baseball—in Allen Craig, their regular-season super-sub and postseason hero in good standing, they had an option at designated hitter that most AL clubs, the Rangers included, would envy. Standing in right field to rest Lance Berkman's balky knees, Craig made a literal impact in his first plate appearance of Game 3, hitting a home run deep to left field off the Rangers' Matt Harrison.

He had gotten the Cardinals on the board, but Game 3 belonged to the game's only two veterans of the 2004 and 2006 World Series. After a rally composed of a missed call at first base, a double, an intentional walk, an error at first base, and a weak Ryan Theriot single to left field gave the Cardinals a 5–3 lead and forced Harrison out of the game, the Cardinals and Rangers traded rallies in the fifth inning. In the top, Yadier Molina's two-run double put the Cardinals at eight runs; in the bottom, Young, Beltre, and Napoli brought the Rangers to within two.

It looked like nobody would ever pull away, but after Ogando finally struck out Craig, the Rangers' worst fears were realized: Albert Pujols woke up. His third home run of the postseason, a three-run shot that seemed to create a vacuum in the Arlington stands, was his most authoritative homer since he'd vaporized Brad Lidge in the 2005 NLCS, a 96-mph fastball he turned on so quickly that Tim McCarver, providing color in the broadcast booth, could only murmur, "Oh my gosh."

In the seventh, the game now 12–6, the Cardinals lineup rolled around again, and if Pujols' first blast hadn't been enough

to put the game out of reach in the Ballpark, his second did the trick—a fly ball deep to center field scored Craig and made the score 14–6. In the ninth inning, down 15–7, the Rangers had no reason not to pitch to Pujols, which is the only reason they did. He responded by becoming the first player in National League history—and the first since Reggie Jackson in 1977—to hit three home runs in a World Series game; he was on his way to going 5–6 with six RBIs.

But the Cardinals' bullpen luck continued to run dry against the Rangers in ways nearly as fantastic as the ones that had put the bullpen in control in the first place. After getting shut out by the Rangers in Game 4 to tie the series at two, the Cardinals found their Game 5 rally foiled by nothing less than the humble bullpen phone.

Tony La Russa attempted to explain it after the game, a 4–2 loss that had seen Marc Rzepczynski and Lance Lynn come into an eighth-inning tie with runners on base instead of Jason Motte. In the post-game conference, La Russa revealed that it hadn't been bullpen hubris that had caused it—it had been something like a wrong number on the antiquated landline phones that adorn dugouts and bullpens across Major League Baseball.

With Dotel struggling in the eighth inning, La Russa had made his first call, asking the bullpen coach to rouse Rzepczynski to face David Murphy and Motte to finish off the eighth inning. Rzepczynski stood up, but Motte's name had been drowned out by the raucous Arlington crowd. When La Russa saw just one silhouette in the left-field bullpen, he made another call, asking for Motte directly; this time bullpen coach Derek Lilliquist heard Lynn's name.

The result was bizarre even by Cardinals postseason standards. Rzepczynski, almost perfect against left-handers, was beaten by lefty masher Mike Napoli, whereupon Lance Lynn came in to face Ian Kinsler and promptly intentionally walked him. With the bases loaded and the damage done, Motte finally arrived to strike out Elvis Andrus.

In Game 6, the Cardinals found themselves under the gun once again with all of their advantages called into question—the bullpen beaten, the offense inconsistent, the starters still struggling. But the Busch Stadium faithful, in Game 6, would be rewarded for their faith by the best game in World Series history.

Nobody's game illustrated the downs and ups of the Cardinals' fortunes as well as St. Louis native David Freese, whose entire brilliant postseason threatened to be eclipsed by an embarrassing fifth-inning error. With Fernando Salas already in the game for Jaime Garcia, Freese had allowed a Josh Hamilton infield fly ball to land no more than a foot behind his back—standing ramrod straight, his glove in the air, he'd simply missed it, as though it had been caught in a high wind. The next batter, Mike Young, broke the 3–3 tie with an RBI double, putting the Cardinals within four innings of elimination.

The Cardinals had been remarkably sloppy all day. Matt Holliday's fourth-inning error, reminiscent of his 2009 NLDS laugher, had allowed the Rangers' third run to score in the same way.

Things continued that way in the seventh inning. In the bottom of the sixth, the Cardinals had gotten a lucky break on a Matt Holliday ground ball and turned it into a bases-loaded walk from Yadier Molina to tie the game back at four. But Lance Lynn, sent in to face the middle of the order in the seventh, was beaten badly—Adrian Beltre and Nelson Cruz homered back to back, and Octavio Dotel was unable to stop the bleeding, giving the Rangers a 7–4 lead with nine outs to go.

In the seventh inning the Cardinals went quietly, but in the eighth inning the Cardinals' unbelievable will to rally showed itself to be undiminished—Allen Craig finally got hold of a Derek Holland pitch, hitting his second home run of the series. But a subsequent rally from the bottom of the order failed, and the Cardinals found themselves down two runs in the bottom of the ninth inning, with Neftali Feliz on the mound.

After Theriot struck out swinging, the Cardinals had to deal with another run of questions about Albert Pujols' future—for the fourth or fifth time, the postseason broadcasters were left to ask whether it'd be Pujols' last at-bat as a Cardinal. Fittingly, he hit a one-out double.

More fittingly still, it wasn't the end at all. Lance Berkman walked on four pitches next, and after an Allen Craig strikeout, the Cardinals were left with none other than David Freese, the NLCS hero and the Game 6 goat, up to bat with two on, two out, and rapidly, two strikes.

Busch Stadium held its breath and prepared to escape a Rangers celebration. Feliz set on a 1–2 pitch. And David Freese did what he'd done all postseason—the ball got deep in the zone, and Freese slammed it on a line into right field. Nelson Cruz leapt for it and fell inches short, the ball skipped over his glove, and by the time anyone dared use the bullpen phone over a wild Cardinals crowd, Freese was at third base, Pujols and Berkman were home, and the Cardinals were tied.

It was a storybook ending, but the game wasn't over yet—with one out in the top of the 10th the Rangers watched as injured team leader Josh Hamilton struck a Jason Motte pitch deep into the stands, seemingly erasing Freese's heroics with one blow. The bottom of the 10th, which pitted the left-handed bottom of the order against a southpaw specialist Rangers manager Ron Washington had sequestered for exactly that occasion, was a quiet affair outside the visitors clubhouse where attendants were rapidly replacing what they'd just finished taking down.

Until reserve infielder Daniel Descalso, who'd earned a reputation for clutch hits at midseason, slapped a ground ball through the hole for a leadoff single. Jon Jay hit a Texas Leaguer at Adrian Beltre. With runners on second and third and nobody left on the bench, Tony La Russa used two starting pitchers in the same at-bat, feinting a pinch-hit with Edwin Jackson before bringing Kyle Lohse in for a sacrifice bunt.

Ryan Theriot's RBI groundout led to a chance for Washington to put into practice what he'd learned in Game 3. Albert Pujols was intentionally walked, loading the bases for Lance Berkman, but this time it didn't work—with the Cardinals again down to their last strike of the season, Berkman singled up the middle, retying the game and sending Busch Stadium into hysterics.

Career World Series Hits

Rank	Player	Year	Hits
1.	Lou Brock	1968	13
2.	Pepper Martin	1931	12
	Lou Brock	1967	12
4.	Ripper Collins	1934	11
	Pepper Martin	1934	
	Joe Medwick	1934	
	Tim McCarver	1964	
	Lance Berkman	2011	
9.	Jim Bottomley	1926	10
	Billy Southworth	1926	
	Tommy Thevenow	1926	
	Roger Maris	1967	
	Willie McGee	1987	

Career World Series Home Runs

Rank	Player	Year	HR
1.	Albert Pujols	2011	3
	Allen Craig	2011	
3.	Rudy York	1946	2
	Ken Boyer	1964	
	Lou Brock	1968	
	Orlando Cepeda	1968	
	Willie McGee	1982	
	Larry Walker	2004	
9.	Others	1926–2011	1

Career World Series Runs Batted In

Rank	Player	Year	RBI
1.	Yadier Molina	2011	9
2.	Keith Hernandez	1982	8
3.	Roger Maris	1967	7
	David Freese	2011	
5.	Les Bell	1926	6
	Jack Rothrock	1934	
	Harry Walker	1946	
	Ken Boyer	1964	
	Orlando Cepeda	1968	
	Albert Pujols	2011	

Everything after that seemed like a dream—Jake Westbrook retired a sleepwalking Rangers rally in the top of the 11th, and stuck once more on a two-strike count, David Freese sent a Mark Lowe pitch into the batters' eye in center field, capping the most incredible individual World Series performance of all time with a game-winner.

Of course it only seemed inevitable in hindsight, but Game 7 that Friday was anticlimax from the beginning. The last clash came in the first inning when adherents to the team-of-destiny theory saw the Rangers methodically put two runs on a shaky Chris Carpenter to start the game. Briefly chastened, they watched as Rangers starter Matt Harrison walked Pujols and Berkman in sequence and was greeted by David Freese, who completed his ascension into Cardinals heaven by hammering a double, tying the game, and using up all the air in the Texas dugout at once.

That was all Chris Carpenter needed to settle, and it was all the Cardinals' offense needed to spin back to life for one more impressive rally. By then the improbable had become routine; by then it was no longer a stretch

Behind the Numbers

WPA, or Win Probability Added, attempts to measure how much a batter or pitcher changes his team's probability of winning or losing a game—a walk with the bases loaded and two out in the bottom of the ninth of a tie game is worth more than a walk with the bases empty in a blowout.

David Freese's World Series Game 6 score of 0.969 is the highest in postseason history, beating out Kirk Gibson's famous 0.870 in Game 1 of the 1988 World Series.

to expect Freese to break every Rangers rally with an extra-base hit; and it was no longer a shock when Allen Craig became the second Cardinal ever to hit three home runs in a World Series.

That was the story of the 2011 Cardinals. By the time Jason Motte got David Murphy to fly out to left field for the last out of their 6–2 win, they'd strung together a season of incredible moments so consistently surprising as to become ordinary. The Cardinals' 11th World Series win was, to the final out, so reliably unlikely that we'd all come to expect it.

ABOUT THE AUTHOR

Dan Moore has been the managing editor of *Viva El Birdos*, the Internet's largest Cardinals weblog, since 2008.

Currently the regional editor of SB Nation St. Louis, he's written about baseball for *Sports Weekly* and the *Wall Street Journal*, and he appears regularly in the Maple Street Press Cardinals Annual.

Dan lives in Springfield, Illinois.